Tom

Peters

REINVENTING WORK

ALFRED A. KNOPF,

NEW YORK 1999

the

project

50

This Is a Borzoi Book
Published by Alfred A. Knopf, Inc.

Copyright © 1999 by Excel/A California Partnership

www.randomhouse.com

Grateful acknowledgment is made to Clarkson N. Potter for
permission to reprint excerpts from *Aha! 10 Ways to Free
Your Creative Spirit & Find Your Great Ideas* by Jordan Ayan.
Copyright © 1997 by Jordan Ayan. Reprinted by permission
of Clarkson N. Potter, a division of Crown Publishers, Inc.

Library of Congress Cataloging-in-Publication Data
Peters, Thomas J.
   The project50: or; transform every "task" into a project
that matters! /.by Tom Peters . — 1st ed.
   p.   cm. — (Reinventing work)
   ISBN 0-375-40773-1
   1. Work—Psychological aspects. 2. Job enrichment.
3. Success—Psychological aspects. I. Title. II. Series.
   BF481.P48   1999
   650.1—dc21   99-33615
                                        CIP

Manufactured in the United States of America
First Edition

DEDICATION

Dick Anderson, former commanding officer, U.S. Naval Mobile Construction Battalion Nine, Danang, Republic of Vietnam, who taught me (Ensign T.J. Peters, CEC, USN 693355) Can Do!*/WOW Projects! in 1966.

James Carville, for "the campaign" as ultimate, high-stakes WOW Project.

Susan Sargent, Perk Perkins, and **The Dream Team,** "true believers" and against-all-odds creators of Hunter Park and Riley Rink, Southern Vermont's most extraordinary community facility.

---

*Fact: The U.S. Navy Seabees' "Can Do!" preceded Nike's "Just Do It!" by 50 years.

What we do matters to us. Work may not be the most important thing in our lives or the only thing. We may work because we must, but we still want to love, to feel pride in, to respect ourselves for what we do and to make a difference. —Sara Ann Friedman, *Work Matters: Women Talk About Their Jobs and Their Lives*

5oLISTS: CREDO

CUBICLE SLAVES ... HACK OFF YOUR TIES ... FLIP OFF YOUR HEELS ...

THE WORK CAN BE COOL!

THE WORK CAN BE BEAUTIFUL!

THE WORK CAN BE FUN!

THE WORK CAN MAKE A DIFFERENCE!

Y-O-U CAN MAKE A DIFFERENCE!

BASH YOUR CUBICLE WALLS!

RIP UP YOUR DILBERT CARTOONS!

THE WHITE COLLAR REVOLUTION IS ON!

90 PERCENT OF OUR JOBS ARE IN JEOPARDY!

TAKE CHARGE OF YOUR LIFE!

SUBVERT THE HIERARCHY!

MAKE EVERY PROJECT A WOW!

BE DISTINCT ... OR EXTINCT!

IT'S A NEW MILLENNIUM: IF NOT NOW ... W-H-E-N?

5 0 L I S T S :
SERIES INTRODUCTION

We aren't knocking Dilbert. Who would dare? But we do believe that work can be cool. THAT THE WORK MATTERS.
—Tom Peters

Work—yours and mine—as we know it today will be reinvented in the next ten years. It's as simple as that. And as profound. Here's why…

The tough old union militant remembers. In 1970 (not exactly an eon ago) it took 108 guys some five days to unload a ship full of timber. And now? Container daze: eight guys…one day.

It happened on the farm when the thresher came along. It happened in the distribution center when the forklift arrived. And it happened dockside.

But, hey, it's the new millennium. Ninety-plus percent of us—even in so-called "manufacturing" companies—work at white collar jobs. Fact: We haven't touched—or really even bothered with—white collar productivity. Never. Until now…

It's a brand-new ballgame. THE WHITE COLLAR REVOLUTION IS ON! The accounting "shop" is coming under the same productivity searchlight that those docks did. And we think we have an inkling of what the new rules will be.

The revolution: Information systems. Information technology. Enterprise Resource Planning systems. Intranets.

Knowledge-capital-management schemes. Enterprise Customer Management. The Web. Globalization. Global deregulation. Etc. Etc. All fueling a—no hype—once every 100, 200, 500(?) years revolution.

Which brings us to this new series of books—which aims at nothing less than a total reinvention of work (how we think about it, undertake it, bring ourselves to it). The work-reinvention revolution turns out to be a matchless opportunity for liberation—in our organizations and in our own lives.

This book is part of the first release in a series of what we call 50Lists. Each book describes a different aspect of work in the New Economy. Each book is built on 50 essential ideas. —The Editors

CONTENTS

II. Sell!

III. Implement!

IV. Exit!

REINVENTING WORK

the project

50

INTRODUCTION:
WHY THE BIG DEAL
ABOUT PROJECTS?

The White Collar Revolution is here. (Finally.) The White Collar Revolution will embrace—ready or not!—90+ percent of workers in the next 10 or so years.

*And most of us are **not** ready.*

It's elementary, my dear Watson. Most white collar jobs—as we know them—will disappear as we get the ERP/Enterprise Resource Planning—etc.—"stuff" right. You read that correctly, colleagues: 90+ percent. Gone. As in: Sayonara. White collar world circa 2004 is going to make "re-engineering" circa 1994 look like very small change indeed.

I've wrestled with this issue for years. Hunting for *an* answer to *the* question: How do today's white collar workers—**you and me!**—transform ourselves, much as yesterday's factory workers and longshoremen did?

THE UN-STUDIED PROFESSIONAL SERVICE
FIRM AS EXEMPLAR

There is a class of organization which has long turned white collar work into something scintillating … and damn profitable. Namely, the professional service firm … or "PSF," as I call it. Lawyers. Architects. Graphic designers. Industrial designers. Engineering service firms. Management consultancies. Accountancies. Ad agencies. Once at the periphery—and seen, frankly, as parasites of the manufacturing-based economy—these outfits are now front and center and role definers in the so-called "knowledge economy."

(Funny thing: We know so little about these firms. About how and why they work. We haven't studied them. I can only guess that's because we didn't take them seriously. We really did see them as parasitic.)

Some are huge … an Andersen (as in Arthur Andersen and Andersen Consulting) … or EDS. They book billions upon billions of dollars a year in revenue. And can employ upwards of 100,000 people. Then there are the one-person professional service firms—the local accountant, say, working from his spare bedroom. But they're all dedicated to the same thing: providing services and making money by leveraging knowledge. **Period.**

My (inexorable?) conclusion? Those who survive—on or off the corporate payroll—will assume the attributes of "real" professional service firm members. And they will behave—again, regardless of their current official status—as independent contractors.

Which leads me … naturally and inevitably … and finally to … **The Work Itself.** Namely, to … **p-r-o-j-e-c-t-s.**

PROJECTS WITH CHARACTER:
THE (ONLY POSSIBLE) (NEW) BOTTOM LINE

The professional service firm—whether it has 2 or 22,222 employees—has an invariant common denominator: the project. Projects—with beginnings and ends and clients and deliverables—are what professional service firms do. **Period.** Join one, and you'll find yourself on a project team by noon of your first day at work. (That was my experience at McKinsey & Co. in December 1974. I arrived at work at 9:00 a.m. By 10 a.m. I was on a project team evaluating a quarter-billion-dollar agrochemical facility. By 1:00 p.m. I was flying to Clinton, Iowa, to visit the Client.) And you'll be on a project team until an hour before you turn in your front-door key and leave for good. (Again, that's the way it went for me at McKinsey in December of 1981. In fact, even after I left I did some contract work on my final project.)

Now, here's the really odd thing: Not only have we not studied professional service firms … but also we haven't studied *projects*. Sure, we have project tools—bar charts, Gantt charts, PERT/CPM (Program Evaluation and Review Technique/Critical Path Method). And a ton of software, such as Microsoft Project.

But: Almost all the work on projects begs the premier issue. What is the "it" of a project? What makes "it" memorable? Or … not-so-memorable?

I've spent 30 years studying business. Took my accounting courses, to be sure. And subscribe to the principles of accounting ... and put stock in those bar charts and PERT diagrams. (My second civil engineering degree is in construction management ... and I learned all the ins and outs of PERT-ing.) But my career has really been devoted to the "other" side of enterprise—the passion, the emotion, the excitement, the dreams, the noble fiascoes. And I firmly believe that this is where the fruits of the emergent White Collar Revolution are to be found.

That is: **The high-impact project is the gem ... the nugget ... the fundamental atomic particle from which the new white collar world will be constructed and/or reconstructed.** My unabashed aim: reinvent the language of projects. (And in the process ... reinvent work!) No, I don't dismiss those software packages. (Though most are far more complicated than necessary. "Great 'groupware,'" one technology exec said to me. "Easy. It's called 'e-mail.'") But I aim to focus in these pages on what I call "the missing 98 percent" ... the "stuff" of creating ... and selling ... and implementing ... projects you'll still be bragging and chortling about ... **10(!)** years from now.

COLLECTING GEMS!

Since I started studying scintillating projects, I've become mesmerized by individuals and groups on quests. E.g.: Just read an article in *The New Yorker* by Jean Strouse, who has written a new biography of J. P. Morgan. Does the world in 1999 really need another "new" biography of this guy? Well, Ms. Strouse reports that she was the first to get access to new material on Morgan. Ta-da: She spent *f-i-v-e y-e-a-r-s* reading it. **Love that! As in: How cool!**

And then there was the first novel, *Raven*, by Peter Landesman. It chronicles the life of Maine lobstermen. (And … what a life.) I was struck by their uniformly magisterial command of their discipline. And their perseverance. *And* struck by how far that was—in this black, unromantic tale—from Dilbert/don't-give-a-shit land.

Not to mention Patrons' opening night, 30 May 1999, at MASS MoCA (Massachusetts Museum of Contemporary Arts). North Adams, Mass., is a classic ex–manufacturing town in decline. Yet through the inspired vision of Guggenheim Museum director Thomas Krens, an abandoned Sprague Electric Company factory—under the guiding hand of architects such as Frank Gehry—has been transformed into the largest center for contemporary visual and performing arts in the United States (13 acres, 27 buildings … 220,000 square feet of galleries, theaters, rehearsal theaters, and art fabrication spaces). Hurdles were numerous … e.g., when the "Massachusetts Miracle" ran dry, state matching funding threatened to run dry as well. In the end, however, an "insane" dream has become a magnificent reality. As the *Wall Street Journal*'s reviewer of the museum's Opening Night put it, "I have seen the future, and it's MASS MoCA."

I.e.: **The Work Can Matter.**

OUR "MODEL"

Our model is simple. And it will be expanded upon in this book and others in this series. To wit:

The "stuff"—Enterprise Resource Planning Systems, Electronic Data Interchange, company intranets, the Web etc.—are fueling a revolution. Point-of-impact for this millennial meteor: the **white collar** worker.

Those who survive—on or off a corporate payroll—will jettison (almost) everything they've learned and adopt the attributes/attitudes of a PSF/**Professional Service Firm.** (See above and our companion book in this series, *the Professional Service Firm50.*) Each will behave as an independent contractor, or what I call **Brand You.** (See our *the Brand You50.*) I.e., survivors will "be" a product ... and exhibit clear-cut distinction at something.

And the bottom line—the base element—for the PSF, Brand You, and the White Collar Revolution: **the Project** (the subject of this book).

That's it. The Three Elements. The organization: **Professional Service Firm.** The individual: **Brand You.** The work: **the Project.** Period.

MISSING-IN-ACTION I: THE PROJECT

I just don't get it! Not long ago I read a terrific book about the new employee-as-businessperson and independent contractor: William Bridges's *Creating You & Company.* I learned a lot ... and in fact have stolen a lot from it (with appropriate attribution). But I recently went back to take a second look. G-r-e-a-t stuff. I was right about that. But guess what: not a word about projects. "Projects" is not even in the index. And yet what is (necessarily) the nub of *You & Company*? *My* take: the project! So why/how did Mr. Bridges miss it? Damned if I know.

Then there is Joel Henning's *The Future of Staff Groups.* Another good and original piece of work. And a rare treatise on this—largely ignored—subject. Index: No "project." W-h-y? (Redux.)

And in the under-studied world of professional service firms there is but one guru: David Maister. I *love* his work! Learn from it! Steal from it again and again (with attribution)! So I went to his latest, *True Professionalism*. Great Stuff. Missing from the index: the project. Again: *Why?* Again: Beats me!

MISSING-IN-ACTION II: THE WORK ITSELF!

We don't need "great leaders." We as individuals need to get on with doing "fabulous stuff," accepting nothing less of ourselves. —Seminar participant, Warsaw (12/98)

Can you imagine a "great" cardiologist who's not obsessed with hearts? —Seminar participant, Zurich (12/98)

It's a funny thing about management books. They rarely talk about the work itself. About the goosebump-inducing projects that staffers are (we hope) engaged in. Sure…"the work" of management is motivation, inspiration, organization, vision. But how can you understand these ideas unless you talk about…**the work itself?**

I guess that's why I fell instantly in love with George Leonard's *Mastery*. Based largely upon his long trek toward judo Black Belt status, the book is about … the work itself. How Leonard progresses to achieve—painstakingly and over a long period of time—exceptional competence at something of merit.

Ponder: It's odd (no?) that no one (!) writes about "achieving greatness at HR work," "exceptional competence at finance." Hmmm…

(Why don't we consider HR as cool as football? The Denver Broncos—and I am a rabid NFL fan—push an inflated pig bladder up and down a field covered with fake grass. The divisional HR director is responsible for, say, the professional development of 623 of her fellow human beings. To me ... she's cooler than John Elway. Okay?)

Why is Silicon Valley so successful? My contention: It's de facto home to the anti-Dilbert movement! That is, an unusually high share of "employees" are caught up in ... The Work Itself. They groove on their mission ... their cool products ... the earth-altering (as they see it) projects they're engaged in. (And they don't mind the stock options—symbols of *real* ownership—either.)

* * *

You have to do stuff that average people don't understand, because those are the only good things. —Andy Warhol

* * *

Blame it all (why not?) on the Harvard Business School ... the one-size-fits-all '70s mentality that "good managers can manage anything." Missing: a passion for "it"—cars, burgers, ads, HR, whatever.

Per our Zurich seminar participant whose quote launched this section—can you imagine a cardiologist without a passion for hearts? A pro baseball player not obsessed with baseball? A great janitor not obsessed with cleanliness?

I can't.

PASSION PLUS

This short book is not about the "passion side" of projects. That's horribly misleading! It suggests 50 percent of project life is "cold" … the bar charts. And 50 percent is "hot" … the passion. That's a dangerous separation … the antithesis of what I'm fighting for … which is integration of *all* aspects of a project into a memorable whole. This is a book about *real* projects and the *real* problems they face:

Challenge 1: Futzing with the structure and specifics of a given task … until it becomes a "way cool project," as one of my co-conspirators puts it.

Challenge 2: Selling that "way cool project." Great project management—in the real world!—turns out to be mostly a sales game. I.e., getting all sorts of folks to support you, help you, give you their very best!

Challenge 3: Execution … more art! Gathering users. Testing stuff on the fly. Always moving … revising … driving … creating momentum. Building buzz … and inevitability … around your project. Completing the project and delivering a WOW result … something you'll be bragging about for years to come.

Challenge 4: And then, finally … letting go … and turning the project over to "the suits" so that it can become part of the mainstream, the new (c-o-o-l) "way we do things around here."

A.K.A. **WOW PROJECTS!**

Ah, yes … **Way Cool**. Let me confess: This *is* a book about Way Cool Projects. (We called it *The Art of the Really Cool Project* at one point.) Our currently favored term: WOW Projects. (I.e.: WOW = Way Cool.) David Ogilvy, the great advertising man, said a memorable ad should "make you gasp." *Nightline* host Ted Koppel refers to really great news stories as "ladle droppers"—meaning that someone cooking in the kitchen would drop the ladle and r-u-n to the TV set. I love that … ladle droppers. Well, I think great—way cool!—projects, such as Apple's Mac (or iMac), Lockheed's SR-71, Gillette's Sensor, MASS MoCA … *and that new training program you're at work on* … should make you gasp … should be a ladle dropper.

Should be … well … **WOW!**

a **WOW** project! is . . . . . .

13

A **WOW** Project!...WOWs.(Period.)

A **WOW** Project! ... is dynamic, stimulating, a major bond builder with co-workers, a source of buzz among end-users, and ... inspiring, exhausting, hot, cool, sexy, where everyone else wants to be.

A **WOW** Project!...confronts and redefines an important issue or problem in such a way that participants (pirates?) will be remembered for it ten years later. ("I was on Apple's original Mac team.") An innovation halo hovers over participant-pirates.

A **WOW** Project!...moves at record speed...is considered a startling success even by early detractors ... makes QuickPrototyping its mantra ... and thumbs its nose at all things bureaucratic.

A **WOW** Project!... is directly "measured" in terms of Beauty + Grace + WOW! + Revolutionary Impact + User Raves.

A **WOW** Project! ... is the place to be! It's the nub of Brand You. If you passed up the chance to be on the team ... well, better luck next time.

A **WOW** Project! ... is the quintessential expression of personality and character. Its demands are heavy. Its returns immeasurable. It is not for the faint-of-heart.

A **WOW** Project!...starts with Y-O-U.

THE PROJECT C'EST MOI!

In the Wayne Wang movie *Smoke*, Auggie (played by Harvey Keitel), a shop owner in Brooklyn, unexpectedly opens up to Paul Benjamin (played by William Hurt), a writer whose wife has been murdered on the streets. He invites Benjamin into his backroom apartment and over a cigar pulls out an imposing pile of photo albums. Auggie, it turns out, has been taking a photo every morning—for years!—at the same street corner at the same time. The albums are moving, to say the least. Auggie confides to Benjamin, "This is my real life's work. This is my *project*."

I love this example. For me, it captures perfectly the essence, the passion, the imperative of t-h-e p-r-o-j-e-c-t. Or, rather: the project-that-really-matters-and-defines-me.

It can be the construction of the Channel Tunnel or the space station. Or it can be photos taken at the same Brooklyn street corner at the same moment every morning…for years.

The common denominator: Something that matters! Something that counts! Something that defines! Something that is imbued with soul. And with life!

It's none of your business, of course, but I admired my then wife-to-be, Susan Sargent, before I loved her. She had drive, gumption, and imagination: She proposed building an Olympic-size hockey rink in a small Vermont town—a rink that could also be used as a statewide center for the performing arts when the ice wasn't down. It was a ludicrous dream. (A five-million-dollar dream in a five-dollar town.) In fact, she and her early cabal members called themselves The Dream Team. For six years they struggled against all odds. Setbacks were numerous. Depression was a staple of life. And yet she and her pirate band prevailed. The rink now stands, and it is definitely a ladle-dropper. She is, incidentally, also a successful artist and entrepreneur. But that rink was her WOW Project. And it is her "defining project."

Can all of one's work life be like that rink? I honestly think so. Obviously, despite hard work and heroic efforts, many dreams don't come true. But if we don't dare to dream and then throw muscle, heart, and soul into making the dream come true, then WOW Projects—and all of the emotional, intellectual, spiritual, and financial riches that they bring—will surely *not* be our lot in life!

Here's to the possibility of WOW! **Okay?**

ORGANIZATION

Our wrestling match around the under-studied idea of projects/projects-that-matter/ WOW Projects led to the identification of four stages:

* Create!
* Sell!
* Implement!
* Exit!

Furthermore, it is my contention that 3 of the 4 stages (all but "implement") are missing in 9 out of 10 (10 out of 10?) tracts on project management. And "they"—the traditionalists—get the implementation part all wrong, too, treating it as a mechanical act ... when it's actually mostly an extension of the selling phase.

Consider:

	CREATE	SELL	IMPLEMENT	EXIT
Traditional				
Emphasis	10%	0%	90%	0%
Our Approach	30%	30%	30%	10%

Our view: Shaping the project **("create")** is all important. I.e.: Is it cool/Is it worth doing? Can it attract cool/maverick adherents?

Hustling **("sell")** is as critical for the effective business-process-redesign project in finance as it is for a Broadway production-to-be.

Execution **("implement")** *is* essential, but we de-emphasize the lengthy plans-on-paper and emphasize the trial-and-error part. (In fact, we think this is so important—what we label Quick Prototyping—that we'll devote an entire book in this series to the topic ... *the Quick Prototype50.*)

And, finally, turnover to the mainstream **("exit")** is also a fine art ... blow it and the project has no lasting impact.

* * *

In the end we aim to do no less than redefine "the project life" ... and in the process take a crack at redefining work itself. Life (organizational, personal) = Projects. Life-well-lived (organizational, personal) = WOW Projects.

THE WOW PROJECT VS. A "DAY AT WORK"

I was in New York for a few days in late January 1999. On Thursday night I went to Carnegie Hall and listened to the Orchestra of St. Luke's, under Sir Charles Mackerras's inspired direction, perform "A Haydn Miscellany." On Friday night I saw the Metropolitan Opera, with Placido Domingo, present a stunning *Simon Boccanegra*. On Saturday morning, at Rizzoli's, I picked up a copy of a book I'd never heard of, Sir Peter Hall's *Cities in Civilization*. Somewhere along the way it occurred to me that each of these "events"/"items" ... performance or tome ... was a WOW Project ... and a long (long) way from a day-in-the-office, Dilbert-flavor.

So what's the difference?

PLACIDO-AT-THE-MET/ETC.	PURCHASING DEPT./ETC.
A performance!	A job.
An act of unbridled passion.	Puttin' in time.
Memorable!	Forgettable.
WOW!	Blah.
A signature piece.	Bureaucratic dross.
The epitome of character.	Faceless.
A plunge into the unknown.	Predictable.
Immediately judicable.	Largely invisible.
The product of enormous investment.	Another day's work.

PLACIDO-AT-THE-MET/ETC.	PURCHASING DEPT./ETC.
Demonstrating mastery of craft.	"Acceptable work."
Exhausting.	Numbing.
Talent rules!	Hierarchy rules.
Energizes the performers.	Enervates the "employees."
Alters the users' universe.	"Customer"-as-afterthought.
Hot.	Tepid.
Technicolor.	Pastel.
Design-centric.	Design-free.
Quirky!	Predictable.
It matters!	Ho-hum.
Reaches out.	Inward-focused.
Adventuresome.	Risk-averse.
Exposed.	Hidden.
Growth experience.	Another day older.
Curious to a fault!	Colors within the lines.
Talent/Craft driven.	Boss-driven. (Suck-up City.)
A beginning and an end.	Un-punctuated.
A plot!	Tune-less.

BRIEF USER'S GUIDE

Ye gads! In the pages that follow, you will find some 200 suggestions. (Things To Do/T.T.D.s.) Many—most?—are labeled "high priority." Most take time—lots of—and concerted effort. And they add up to enough work for a fully staffed platoon.

So ... what's realistic? We've been using this "stuff" with seminar participants for over a year now. It has worked for others, so I recommend that you use it as they have.

The book is broken into 50+ items that appear in four sections. (Section IV is short.) So ...

1. Go through the sections one at a time. Pick your top four items from sections one, two, and three. (And pick one from section four.) Basis: Stuff that seems important. Stuff you're currently overlooking. Stuff that's oddball but may be worth a look.

2. Now examine the action items associated with each of your selections. Pick one action item per selection worth cranking on now. (Per the metric above, that'll give you about 13 action items.)

3. Take that list of 13, and put priorities against them: 1 = Gotta Do. 2 = Great Idea. 3 = Good idea, but not as useful/cool as the others.

4. Get to work on three or four of the highest priorities from the examination in step three above.

There's no genius to this. Most of you will underline some things that resonate for you ... and then get to work as you see fit. That's fine and dandy. And works fine. Our little drill is just a logjam breaker if you get stuck.

Also, our "drill" will work if a Team is processing this material. Again, it's not genius; it is a way to spur somewhat structured discussion.

(**Caution:** It's very easy to pick the comfortable suggestions. P-l-e-a-s-e ... make sure that close to half of your priorities could be classified as "surprising." That is, they push you—and your colleagues—to uncomfortable spaces and places.)

* * *

Good Luck!
Have Fun!

I. create!

I. What's with this so-called "inventing"/
"finding" a WOW Project? You get an
assignment, right?

Your spouse says, "Fix the toilet. Now."

And the boss says, "Let's redesign the Returns Policy
to be a little less bureaucratic."

Each one is a "project." Each one is pretty damn clear.

W r o n g .   E x a c t l y   w r o n g .

The toilet job? Should we fix the toilet? Sure. But it
also brings up the fact that the bathroom is in the wrong
damn place! (Can't believe what idiots the people were
who designed and built this house.) Maybe we really
ought to get moving with that oft-delayed renovation
project. Which reminds me, my mom is getting older,
older, older. We really should think about building an "in-
law" apartment for her over the garage. Etc.

And the Returns Policy? Is it really just a "tidy-up-the-language" project? That's not a bad idea. But isn't it a fact that the problems with the "mere" Returns Policy reveal: (1) a general excess of bureaucracy and convoluted business processes; (2) an implicit customer-as-inconvenience bias; and (3) mistrust of our own front-line people who must carry out the policy? Couldn't this "little project"—if approached properly—be the thin end of the wedge that leads to a *Culture 2002 Program*, one that attacks our long-standing strategic deficiencies (which are becoming ever more evident as the competition heats up)?

Now, you see—I hope—why I contend that creating and shaping a project is anything but automatically "accepting an assignment."

* * *

He took every opportunity to redefine [a project] brief so that the problem could be solved according to his vision. —Steven Heller, *Paul Rand* (a biography of the pioneer American designer)

The reasonable man adapts himself to the world; the unreasonable man persists in trying to adapt the world to himself. Therefore all progress depends on the unreasonable man.
—George Bernard Shaw, *Man and Superman*

project

50

>>>>>>>

1.

The world of WOW Projects rests on but one word: **REFRAMING**. That is ... every "assignment"/"task"/ "job" is merely a starting point. Your real "job": Turn that—often apparently mundane—task/job/assignment into something cool/memorable/WOW! Repeat after me: I will resist the status quo ... come Hell *and* high water (and resist a boss who just does not *get it*)!

On time. On budget. Who cares?
> —Seminar participant, Houston, Fall 1998,
> on projects that fail to stir the soul

The Nub

WHAT ARE WE UP TO HERE? CREATING STUFF WE'LL REMEMBER ... YEARS FROM NOW.

Recall: My wife Susan led that "impossible" community project to fruition; she'll remember it—vividly—25 years from now. My "big" project at McKinsey & Co.—as well as the first bridge I designed/built as a Navy Seabee in Vietnam—lingers fondly in my mind three decades later.

But to get to that memorable "there" ... you must never, ever accept an assignment as given! Gary Withers, chief of the brilliant British marketing firm Imagination

Ltd., agrees to help two companies get beyond post-merger blues. He ends up inventing a "coming together" party ... for 40,000 people! That is, he took on a routine-ish (dull-ish?) assignment ... and refused to be boxed in by it. He re-invented it. Big time.

The word—rather, T-H-E word—is **REFRAMING. Taking a task—any damn task—and turning it into something-that-makes-a-difference.**

As with most (important) things in life, it's all about attitude and art; i.e., a congenital unwillingness to be painted into a dull corner. An unwillingness to paint with the same old palette. An unwillingness to limit your imagination to the size of the canvas.

You're "in charge" of the company Memorial Day picnic: (1) Poor you? (2) Ho-hum? *Or:* Make it the most incredible, awesome, memorable, high-involvement celebration (project) of "Who we are" and "What we stand for" and "How we care about our people." Ever. Hey: **WHY-THE-HELL-NOT!?**

NO DAMN J.A.M.S.

Phil Daniels attended a seminar I gave in Sydney. I spoke of the "failure imperative": i.e., no failure, no innovation. He went me one better and explained his management philosophy:

"Reward excellent failures."

"Punish mediocre successes."

Yikes! That's rumbled through my head a hundred times. (A hundred hundred times is really more like it. **No joke.**)

The question:
How about that project you're working on ... right now? Headed for WOW? Or more likely ... a "mediocre success" in the making?

Mediocre success: Not shameful. Not a sign of inferior intelligence. Or (necessarily) limited effort. Just ... well ... damn unlikely to be remembered-with-pride five years from now.

After a recent address I gave to managers of a giant financial services company, the CEO took me aside and said, "You really got to me. We are, of course, an information systems company! And I'll bet that 90 percent of our projects take on a life of their own, stagger through to completion, do no harm, but are clearly no more than 'mediocre successes!'"

Rule: Say it. Shout it. Live it.

Just scream "No" to J.A.M.S.

(**J**ust **A**nother **M**ediocre **S**uccess.)

* * *

Before a [Bob Dylan] show in Portland I spoke with a level-headed twenty-something guy who plays in a progressive funk group. "Last time I saw [Dylan], in '90, it was brutal," he told me. "I hope he doesn't f--- up the songs again. I hear he's better. Even when he's awful, he's sort of great—he's never just mediocre."

—Alex Ross, The New Yorker

T.T.D. (Things To Do) / Reframe!

1. Write a one-page description of your current project ... as given. Fax/e-mail it to three or four "cool people" in your Rolodex ... today ... and ask them to help you rethink/reframe it.

2. Set up a meeting—in the next 48 hours—with the **coolest person** in the project's customer group. Ask her what she would do if you turned the project over to her today.

3. Get three or four (no more) pals/teammates together ... today ... for at least an hour ... and brainstorm a new version of the project. (Opening assumption: We'll throw the old definition out ... and start with a blank sheet of paper.) Schedule four more brainstorming meetings—at least two offsite—in the next ten working days.

4. Send the youngest—or oldest or weirdest—member of the team off on a three-day "reinvention sabbatical." Ask him to consult with anybody and everybody ... and next week present a New Look to the whole team.

5. Make an extensive table of project "deliverables." **Label one column "as requested." Create another column labeled "could be." Make each "could be" wild *and* woolly!** (Work with the whole team on this.)

6. What are the "cultural"/"how-we-do-business" assumptions—about customers, people, technology, etc.—that underpin the project's deliverables? **CAN WE FUTZ WITH THEM?** (Talk to the strangest birds you know—in or out of the organization—about this.)

2.

(Or "D.S.C.S."—Doing Seriously Cool Shit...as one pal of mine puts it.) It all starts with keeping your antennae perpetually twitching: e.g., what's bugging, intriguing, exciting you? Start an "Observations Notebook"—paper or electronic. Jot down stuff you come across that is: (1) dumb (no matter how "tiny"/"mundane"—e.g., a user-unfriendly form, an annoyingly obtuse procedure/pro-cedural document); or (2) great stuff that happens in "real life" (at a restaurant, at a ballpark, at the dentist's office) that your operation can learn from.

BIG IDEA: BECOME AN "OBSERVATION FREAK" ... OF THE GOOD, THE VERY GOOD, THE *AWESOME*, THE UGLY, AND THE *AWFUL*.

STEP NO. 1 TO WOW PROJECT POWER: AWARENESS!

The Nub

Winston Churchill said that appetite was the most im-portant thing about education. Leadership guru Warren Bennis says he wants to be remembered as "curious to the end." David Ogilvy contends that the greatest ad copywriters are marked by an insatiable curiosity "about every subject under the sun."

So, too, great project reframers!

The good news: **Curiosity can (more or less) be trained/learned.** My best friend—my wife, actually—is one of a number of "notebook freaks" I know. When she's on a product-sourcing trip for her home-furnishings business, for instance, she'll fill 40 pages of a notebook (she copied this habit from her adored grandfather). There will be notes…and sketches…and pasted-in articles and ads from newspapers or magazines. Likewise, my friend and business guru Karl Weick carries a packet of 3 x 5-inch cards in his inside sport coat pocket: I've never seen him go more than 20 minutes—literally!—without jotting down some observation or other. Another pal writes on matchbook covers, cocktail napkins—and stuffs the little scraps into his left (always left!) pocket; he cleans out the pocket, he reports, every few days … and types the notes, with some elaboration, into an ongoing computer file.

It boils down to studenthood-in-perpetuity/curiosity-in-perpetuity/applied-fanatic restlessness. **That is, a belief that life is … ONE BIG LEARNING EXPERIENCE.** Something mysterious happens to a curious, fully engaged mind—and it happens, as often as not, sub-consciously. Strange little sparks are set off, connections made, insights triggered. The result: an exponentially increased ability to tune up/reinvent/WOW-ize *today*'s project at work!

CURIOSITY CAPERS

Milliken and Co. chairman Roger Milliken: On the job for 50 years, he sits through a meeting, listening like a submarine commander. Meeting ends. Five minutes later,

I observe Roger pacing in the parking lot, dictating machine in hand, noting his observations—and almost immediately translating these into "things to do."

* * *

Yours truly: I take a mass of notes—perhaps 20 pages—while listening to a two-hour presentation. In the next half hour I religiously retreat for a couple of minutes (literally) and distill these into summary points on a single 5 x 7-inch index card.

* * *

Jennifer Hansen, Hansen Design: "To keep myself focused at the beginning of a project, I start a small journal specifically for that job.... I jot my ideas for [that] project, whether a few words or a simple sketch, in [that] journal. I also tape and staple a lot of ... article clippings and photocopies.... I also use these journals to keep notes from client phone calls and meetings. I keep this record with me until the close of the project—it's a great reference tool."

JOURNAL POWER!

From *Aha!,* by Jordan Ayan:

"Creative thinkers ranging from the inventors Thomas Edison, Benjamin Franklin, and Leonardo da Vinci to the novelist Virginia Woolf, the psychologist Carl Jung, and the naturalist Charles Darwin all have used journals and notebooks to record their ideas and inspirations. These people understood that new ideas often come from combining many disparate pieces of information or concepts over an extended period of time. The only effective way to track your ideas and synthesize them is to document them as soon as they bubble up in your mind....

"One of the easiest and most effective ways to record your ideas is to start a personal 'idea journal.' By keeping this journal near you at all times—on top of your desk, in your briefcase or purse, on the kitchen counter, on the nightstand by your bed—you can record ideas that flash through your mind during the day and even at night....

"Whatever form your journal-keeping takes, the most surefire way to murder your impulse to use it is imposing a set of meaningless rules or guidelines. For example, don't feel that your journal is worthless if you don't write in it every day, or if you don't use full, grammatically correct sentences. This is nonsense....

"Use whatever journaling method works for you. One of the best methods I've heard about was developed by a manager at Boeing who wanted to track ideas he had while traveling. He carried pre-addressed, stamped postcards with him on which he wrote ideas as they hit him. Then he mailed the cards back to his house. I also know people who call their voice-mail boxes and leave themselves messages. And tiny tape recorders that will capture a spoken line or two are available inexpensively. There is no end to the clever (and creative) ways you can record and document your ideas."

TOM COMMENT: Strong...and important...stuff! Put this book down. **Right now.** (But please pick it up again later!) Go out and buy yourself a journal—or start on the nearest scrap of paper—and make your first observation. It could well be one of the most important steps of your entire career. (P.S. I'm not exaggerating!)

T.T.D./Awareness

1. Buy a simple spiral-bound notebook. TODAY. Label the front cover "Cool." Label the back cover "Awful."

START RECORDING. TODAY.

2. Wander the local mall ... **TODAY** ... for one hour. Write down 10 "cool" and 10 "awful" observations: great (and awful) service, signage, merchandise, food, restrooms, decor, music, whatever.

3. Record these observations on your computer. **Translate four of them to your current project.**

4. Work with one or two pals on this. Start an **OBSERVATIONS FANATICS TEAM.** Share your "data" ... and translate your insights/observations to your project(s).

2a.

BECOME A BENCHMARKING FOOL: LOOK AT EVERY-SMALL-THING-THAT-HAPPENS-TO-YOU AS A GOLDEN LEARNING OPPORTUNITY.

If something great occurs at the hardware store on Saturday, call the store owner up on Monday and ask her to lunch for a Brain-Picking Session. Collect Neat Experiences! Collect Cool People! Turn them into your Personal University faculty!

The Nub

My best friends (is it why they're my best friends?) all "collect cool people." Or, in my preferred jargon—freaks!

One of them, Allen Puckett, who oversaw my early development at McKinsey & Co., would read a stimulating article in some obscure business or scientific journal. He'd call the author out of the blue ... and invite him/her to dinner. In many cases, the author would accept! "Another 'faculty member' for my Personal University," Allen would exclaim. And the next time he was stuck with a thorny/intriguing project, he'd call the newest of his "faculty members," and ask her take on it.

LIFE IS ACTUALLY BRIMMING WITH COOL EXPERIENCES AND THE COOL PEOPLE WHO MAKE THEM HAPPEN. And "all" it takes to tap into that network is a little bit of nerve. I've learned that—surprise!—people love to be taken seriously. If you *love* your restaurant experience this Saturday evening ... and ask the restaurateur to come talk to your band of accountants about service ... I'll bet you 3 to 1 she/he comes ... gleefully. In any event, you'll never know until you try. Right?

MORE COLLECTING COOL

Federal Express founder Fred Smith, to yours truly: "Who is the most interesting person you've met in the last 90 days? Do you suggest I call him or her? If so, how about a phone number?"

Good "trick," Fred!

Jordan Ayan, *Aha!* (again):

"Call one of your creative acquaintances. Find out what he or she is thinking right now. Get inspired from the sharing. If possible, set up a time to visit....

"Think of the one person with whom you'd like most to talk but who you have been afraid to approach. How might you reach this person? What are your fears or hesitations about calling him or her?"

This is great...and serious...wisdom! The planet is full of fabulous minds, ripe for the picking. Start—today—building your personal YOUniversity. CoolU?

T.T.D. / Conscious Collector of Cool!

1. *Write up* at least *three neat experiences* ... in the next *two weeks.*

P-L-E-A-S-E.

2. Call the person responsible for *one* of these neat experiences. Ask her (him) if you can host lunch...and do some brain-picking.

3. Consider ... starting a discussion group ("Cool Business"?) which brings these clever acquaintances of yours together once a month to swap great (and grim) tales.

4. Get *three* of your best pals to join you in the Collection of Cool People.

5. Call someone on your "cool list" ... TODAY ... and get his/her take on your current project. And/or invite her/him to sit down with your group for an hour or two later this week.

3.

Evaluate every-last-experience—filling out an application form for your kid's summer camp—as an **A**wareness **E**xercise: e.g., is that *form* a "WOW!!"? (No kidding … *damn it!*)

The Nub

Hey … this *is* a really big deal. As in … it's-the-whole-point-of-the-exercise. I.e.:

CAN YOU "LEARN" TO (ROUTINELY) USE … AND **LIVE** … THE WORD **WOW**?

The idea: memorable/braggable/WOW Projects. I contend you won't get there—period—unless you can accept "the word" … and the concept … and the *need* for … WOW. (Or: memorable … cool … rockin'… braggable … **insanely great**—the latter from Apple's Steve Jobs.)

But it's even a bigger deal than that: Can you tune in to the WOW Channel … daily? Can you develop your personal WOW-O-Meter? In your most routine affairs? You're filling out a form or buying something at a Web site: Is the process dreary … or Okay … or **WOW**? (How so? How no?) Try to imagine a "WOW" way of doing things … any thing(s).

I went to a huge trade show in North Carolina recently. The show itself was extremely good. But the parking/transportation situation was awful. (Which cast a big negative pall over the whole event.) I awoke one morning … at 3:00 a.m. (yes, I am that obsessed) … and wondered "How do you get to WOW" on the transportation dimension of this otherwise superb event?

IN SHORT, I HAVE CONSCIOUSLY TRAINED MY-SELF IN **WOW.**

I perpetually wonder how any-and-every-experience could be transformed into a memorable/WOW experience. I sincerely believe that using the word—i.e., WOW—is essential!

THE "W-WORD" ITSELF

I recently spoke to the top managers of a property-management company. My topic: WOW Projects. A participant reported that during a subsequent discussion of a proposed program, someone butted in at one point and demanded, "But is this 'WOW' enough?"

Y-e-s!

And … a seminar participant in the media business reports (May 1999): "As we were closing a major piece of business with one of Charlotte's (N. Car.) major banks, the client asked me what kind of value added they could get for placing such an order. My response, instead of telling them what I could do, was, 'What would make you say WOW?' Not only did we get the business, but they got what they really wanted. I have subsequently used that line a number of times, each time with the same squeal of delight from the client."

Again: **Y - E - S !**

WOW AND NON-WOW

A 1998 *Fortune* global survey of "most admired" corporations distinguished between the league leaders … and those who weren't. The magazine declared that among the also-rans "the top priorities were minimizing risk, respecting the chain of command, supporting the boss, and making budget."

Likewise, I recently ran across a book called *The Project Office*. It described project Nirvana as "on time, within budget and according to specifications." That contrasted—rudely—with another book I was coincidentally reading at the same time, the sober *Creating Modern Capitalism*. Author Thomas McCraw, a Harvard economist, summarized, "Capitalism is best understood as an expression of human creativity … propelled by dreams and aspirations."

ATTRIBUTES OF THOSE WHO "MADE" THE 10TH GRADE HISTORY BOOK

History books are not flawless. Or free of controversy. Nonetheless, they represent a sort of "societal consensus" about what/who is important. So…who makes it into the Big Hall of Fame? into your daughter's tenth grade history text? Roosevelt. King. Kennedy(s). Galileo. Einstein. Etc. And traits they share—more or less—in common? Try these:

* Committed.

* Determined to Make a Difference.

* Focused.

* Passionate!

* Risk Seekers.

* Irrational about the righteousness of their life's project.

* Ahead of their time./*Paradigm Busters!*

* Impatient. (But, paradoxically, prepared to stay the course.)

* Action-Obsessed! (Mantra: Ready. *Fire!* Aim.)

* Made *l-o-t-s* of people mad!

* Creative./Quirky./Peculiar.

* Rebels. (Scientists and artists, as well as social-political types.)

* *In The Establishment's face.*/Flouted the chain of command.

* Irreverent./Disrespectful.

- Masters of Improvisation./Thrive on Chaos./ *E-x-p-l-o-i-t Chaos!*

- Ask Forgiveness > Seek Permission.

- Bone Honest!

- Flawed. (Big pluses, big minuses.)

- "Tuned into" followers' needs and aspirations.

- Absurdly good at what they do!

Add it up, and it's my definition of ... WOW! And WOW-ers. And, alas, a portrait of what's missing—or, worse yet, condemned—in most organizations/ departments. No?

So: ponder it. If it's good enough for this ultimate Hall of Fame, the history book, why ain't it good enough for our finance department?

NOT IN THE CHANGE BUSINESS!

We're not in the change business! Sounds nutty, eh? But it's true.

A colleague took me on, comparing me to her ex-husband: "Telling people to 'Do WOW,' " she said, "is like telling a depressed person to 'Get over it and cheer up.' " I take her point. But she misses mine.

I'm not aiming to "WOW up" anyone. It's more like this: Though we're not all Emma Thompsons, I firmly believe that just about everyone has a fair amount of WOW in him or her. It's an integral part of being human. That is ... spirit, spark, passion, creativity ... is natural. Young kids think they can do anything. Their imaginations are unbridled. Unfortunately, the process of growing up, going to school, and learning (?) often teaches us what we *can't* do (MBA programs get special kudos in this Dubious Distinction Department!) and dampens our innate spirit. What I want to do is no more (*and* no less) than give you—and your mates—permission to get in touch with your innate WOW-ness, to *think* WOW, to *try* WOW ... and, upon occasion, to *do* WOW.

In short:

* You'll never know until you try!
* You'll *never* get to WOW unless you are at least willing to aspire to it.

I ache....

I ache when, as at dinner with the top man at a European office of a big professional service firm, I hear over and over ... why he and his company can't "go for it." Rationalizations pour out of him. The corporate controller *this*. The client *that*. (P.S.: It is an ad agency!?)

I'm sad. **So sad.** *And* I've lost patience: If you're not "going for it" now ... when, then? "Next time"?

I've worked in giant companies. I understand the perils of pissing off the powers that be. But ... still ... it's *your* life! And you will remember (in 15 years) only the WOWs—

or the attempted WOWs. How wretched to reach 60 and look back on a life of "good work." "Professional"...yes. "Memorable"...never.

Ye gads!

* * *

I—for one—don't want an epitaph on my tombstone like this:

T.T.D./The "W" (WOW) Word

1. Think back to your very latest retail experience... dry cleaner, restaurant, shoe store, or Radio Shack. Was it a...WOW? How *might* it have been? What happens when you think of such experiences in terms of "WOW" and non-WOW? (Hint: *The* key is *extreme/precise* language: "WOW"… or "blah"… or "shitty.")

2. In the next 48 hours consciously evaluate, say, *every* retail experience on a 1-to-10 Awful-to-WOW Scale. Did any reach no-baloney "WOW"/10? If so: *Why?* Or: *How?* **(Exactly. Ten reasons.)** If not, *why* not? (Exactly. Ten reasons.) And if one experience made it to 8 on that WOW Scale… what might have happened to turn it into a perfect-WOW/10?

3. Get two or three pals to join you in the W-Word Crusade: i.e., evaluating common experiences on an Awful-to-WOW Scale.

4. Get three colleagues together. Spend an hour—or two—talking about the meaning of WOW. (And why we don't use The Word in business.)

5. At your next meeting, ask at least once: "BUT IS THAT **WOW**?"

A M E N   C O R N E R !

I would rather have a smaller number of people be passionate about [my movies] than a big blob of people being so-so about them.   —Terry Gilliam, **director**

4.

Don't assume that "the annoying little snafu" is little. Assume instead that it's the tip of a *Titanic*-ripping iceberg.

AS A MATTER OF HABIT, NEVER LET ANY LOUSY LITTLE THING PASS UNNOTICED.

God—AND A WOW PROJECT—is in the details!

The Nub

Banish the word "little" from your vocabulary! There are no "little" problems. There are only "little" outcroppings ... of b-i-g phenomena.

Am I trying to say there are no molehills, only mountains? To some (large) extent ... yes.

At first glance, the job seems trivial: Tidy up some loose ends in a "comp-time" policy. Well ... you can do that ... "tidy up" those loose ends. Or ... you can research the Hell out of comp-time issues at interesting companies in your industry/city. And you can look at the comp-time issue/policy as one small-ish outcropping of "our basic approach to treating/empowering people." That is, the "little" policy rewrite *can* become—with imagination and persistence—the first roll of the snowball that will alter corporate culture and make ours a "terrific place to work."

Okay, that sounds pretty grand. But why not? The truth is, most exceptional products—from Disneyland to Post-It notes to Baby Joggers to Quicken to Gap Kids—were created to scratch little personal itches. (Walt Disney is said to have wanted a place to take his grandkids. 3M's Post-It man, Art Fry, was tired of having the little scraps of paper he placed in his hymnal to mark the day's selections slip to the floor. Etc.)

The bigger idea: Mindset! **I.e., always look to cast a wider/weirder/deeper net.** It can—**invariably**—be done. It's about building outwards … from the so-called little itch/problem/project … to the big picture/solution/WOW (e.g., Walt and his Kingdom). That little problem/project does not exist in a vacuum; it's your key to entering The Wild World of WOW! (And: Doing so, no matter how junior/"unempowered.")

PROJECT DNA

"CULTURE CHANGE"—THAT BIG, ELUSIVE GOAL— OFTEN STARTS WITH A SINGLE, SMALL WOW PROJECT.

Why? How?

Simple. **Every "small" project contains the entire strand of organizational DNA!** The "small" effort to revise the sick-leave policy reveals—if you are tuned in—the genetic/cultural code as pertains to employees, trust, caring, leadership, basically the whole shebang. Reorder that single strand, and the ripple effect may well alter the organization's entire genetic makeup—for the vigilant WOW-er.

Message: **To get going on a B-I-G issue (like culture change), you do not need a big project.**

In fact there are perils to the big project: It brings to a rapid boil the often contentious "cultural debate." By contrast, the small project allows one to ease into B-I-G change without triggering alarms and setting off a full array of warning lights. By building a miniature model woven of strands of WOW-infused genetic material ... a.k.a. your so-called little project ... you can *prove* to your organization, one "small" but cool step at a time, that there is a better-rockin' way. (Hint: This is precisely why so many successful large-scale-change programs start with an innocent project.)

To raise the ante another notch in the organization, let's consider a unit boss's agenda: Let's say she has 23 people working for her ... engaged in seven projects. Key idea: Treat the seven projects as an integrated portfolio. Turn each of them into "small" WOW Projects that are nonetheless harbingers of big-scale change, or even revolution. Each of the seven becomes, in effect, a prototype for the major change initiative. As usual (hey, it's the whole point) we are using the project—specifically the **Small WOW Project**—as the grist for the b-i-g change mill. The small-WOW-Projects (collectively) provide:

* Low-visibility tests in hidden corners

* Rapid prototyping opportunities

* Experimentation with multiple strategies on a relatively small budget

T.T.D./No Such Thing as "Little!"

1. Examine today's little task(s). (EVERY "LITTLE" TASK!) What are the *unspoken* assumptions behind a form, a policy, whatever? Make a table: "What *is*," and "What's *implied*." Do not rest until you get this right: There are always numerous cultural-political-strategic assumptions embedded in the most "trivial" of activities.

2. Always head directly to the "user." (*And* the user's user. Etc.) *Who* uses this form/procedure? *How? When? Why? What* bugs users? *How* could it be better? *What* is the bigger picture (attitude) of which this is a tiny part? Sign up a couple of users to help you. (You'll make lifelong friends!)

3. Do some Web research. It's pretty much possible, on *any* topic. Search for anything that relates/links to your "little" problem. The goal: to cast a wider/more intriguing net.

4. Prepare two 5 x 7-inch cards: "The Task" (what is), "The Dream"(what could be). Working with users and other cool colleagues, redraft "The Dream" card until something Cool/WOW/Profound ... to you ... and them ... emerges.

5. MAKE THIS APPROACH ("LITTLE" AIN'T!) A STAPLE OF YOUR WORKING—WOW PROJECT— LIFE!

4a.

Any activity—literally!—can be converted to a "WOW."

AND IF YOU THINK I'M EXAGGERATING … YOU'VE TUNED IN TO THE WRONG CHANNEL!

The Nub

Winners—no kidding—**adore crummy jobs!**

Why? Because those jobs allow lots—and lots!—of space. Nobody cares! Nobody is watching! You're on your own! You are King! You can get your hands dirty … make mistakes … take risks … perform miracles!

A friend at McKinsey & Co., Bill Matassoni, turned an unwanted library "cleanup" chore into the thin end of a wedge that led to a wholesale revision of the firm's approach to knowledge accumulation and sharing; the dreary task ended up creating a genuine, new "core competence" at the giant company. His secrets: (1) a congenital unwillingness to let a crappy task drag him down; (2) an unslakable thirst for new learning that allowed him to recast a rotten job into a career-building win.

There is a more general force at work here: The most common lament of the "unempowered" is that they don't have "the space" to do anything cool. To which I unfailingly reply: **Rubbish!**

(Actually, my term is far stronger.) The space *is* there. Most just choose not to use it. Task for all those whiners: Find something "little" (with big consequences) at work that bugs you ... and others ... and figure out how it can be fixed. Then ... go ahead and actually fix it ... on your own time and initiative. Remember: If you see a pile of horseshit—there must be a pony.

Bottom line: Relish the "little" assignment or "chore" that no one else wants! **(SEEK IT OUT!)** It's a license for self-empowerment, whether it's the redesign of a form or planning the weekend client retreat. With verve ... you can turn it into something grand and glorious ... and WOW! ... *always! (A-L-W-A-Y-S!) (Repeat: ALWAYS.) (Now y-o-u repeat: ALWAYS!)*

POWERLESS RULES!

At a recent seminar, we were talking about WOW Projects and front-line folks. And a savvy participant piped up, **"You're never so powerful as when you're powerless."**

Love it.

The "powerless" person is not under the magnifying glass that the department head's job brings. The "powerless" person can take the (little) task—that no one cares that much about—and twist it 'til she's made it a Dramatic Statement...about the company...work...herself ...and, of course...WOW. The "powerless" person, through passion for an idea, can recruit fellow "powerless" sorts ...can mount in effect a Children's Crusade.

The apogee of my on-payroll career came via the project at McKinsey & Co. that led to *In Search of Excellence.* It was clearly—again, in retrospect—the byproduct of power-less-ness. Alas, I'll never be so naïve—and hence so power*ful*—again!

RAISON D'ÊTRE

*In a way, this item is the main reason I wrote this book. I was beleaguered by people at my seminars. "Your message is great," they'd say, "**if I were a VP.** But I'm a little cog in the big wheel. Whaddabout me?!" My answer: I fervently believe the WOW Project is available to a-l-l of us.*

Available, per this entry on the *50List,* **in the tiniest of projects ... if our heads are screwed on right**...that is to say...opportunistically.

T.T.D./The Unmitigated Joy of Crummy Chores!

1. Volunteer for crap! *Today! Now!* **Joyously!** Stymied by a current project? At the next committee meeting, eagerly volunteer for the stupidest task on the boss's project/crappy chore list.

2. Bigger deal: A four-month-long dog of an assignment comes along—to go to the deep boonies to participate in busywork implementation of a new, bug-riddled system. Lousy location. Dreary chore. NO ONE'LL TOUCH IT.

Hooray! **(Don't giggle out loud.)** Just the chance you've been looking for—to be on your own ... and to sparkle by turning the bullshit-mop-up-implementation job into a new "strategic" approach to rolling out/debugging systems ... throughout the entire division.

3. And: **Always** volunteer to be (1) the note-taker, (2) the to-do list creator/manager, (3) the meeting organizer. Nobody wants these jobs—and yet they can turn you, instantly, into de facto project manager ... and be the Gateway to WOW.

* * *

MANTRA(S): **IN CRAP LIES WOW!**
V.F.R.J.: Volunteer for Rotten Jobs. (Or your own words to that effect.)

No Non-WOW!

"But surely," the London seminar participant mused, "not *every* project can be a 'WOW!' Some must be routine?" I pondered a while before answering. But I think my reply was correct: "Nuts! Anything—or project—can be WOW-ed."

And I believe it. Unabashedly so, upon reflection.

Are some projects "smaller" than others? **Of course!** But so what? Think back to age four, that week on the beach at Cape May. The day you were burned to a crisp by the July sun, because you were so damn intent upon making that sand castle the best ever … on making it a … **WOW!**

The task assigned to the teenagers hired for the summer is to clean up the storage area. They do the job "well"? Fine! They leave the place "spotless." Great! But then one kid—the future entrepreneur, I bet—thinks it silly that so many pallets are being scrapped. *What if* they were disassembled and sold? *What if* the loading dock crew offered them to contractors or D.I.Y. hobbyists in need of a pallet or two?

Soon our Budding Billy Gates has actually turned the tons of detritus the storage yard produces into a micro business which, incidentally, also results in a perpetually tidy space.

You've seen it. I've seen it. The 18-year-old … or the 46-year-old … or the 88-year-old … who can't help but turn a project, no matter how small, into a Crusade.

Un-WOW-able? I don't believe it! Your job as boss: Set the tone. Encourage the innovative … everywhere … all the time.

Message:

Stomp out WOW-less-ness! WOW-less-ness is a state of mind!

5.

The two-week project/task to revise an invoicing process or set up a key-account tracking program:

IS IT AN HONEST-TO-JOHN,
NO-BALONEY WOW?

Will you be able to brag about it a year from now or submit a little article about it to your regional professional trade magazine—or at least submit a little article about it to your division's newsletter?

Test:
Write up a two-paragraph summary of the project or a mock press release—right now—and imagine you're submitting it to the newsletter/trade rag:

IS THERE ANYTHING "WOW!" TO SAY?
How do you know it's a "WOW"?

First, ask yourself the basic question: IS THIS A WOW … for *me*? Next, start asking your teammates and your customer the exact same question:

WILL THE RESULTS OF THIS
PROJECT BE
MEMORABLE/BRAGGABLE/"WOW!"?

The Nub

It's the "nanosecond '90s." Soon it'll be the Speed-of-Light 21st Century. Speed is life! The sine qua non of business success. Run ... for your (professional) life ... *fasterfasterfaster.* Etc. We've heard 'em all a thousand times.

So how do you explain Gillette? It reinvented men's shaving, in the spring of 1998. The WOW? Gillette's MACH3. Development time: seven *y-e-a-r-s.* (Yes ... for a "mere" razor.)

No, I'm not suggesting you drag your current project out for seven years. I *am* suggesting that WOW is a big ... serious ... profound ... deal. And sometimes big-serious-profound deals take t-i-m-e. You can't necessarily rush WOW because cut corners and WOW Work are absolutely contradictory.

I want you to remember—fondly and with pride—your current project. F-i-v-e years from now. Maybe t-e-n. Which means it's got to be no-kidding special. Which may mean it gets reframed/reworked/revised a half dozen times ... and ends up taking four months instead of four weeks. (And all the powers-that-be are pissed—at *you*—over the delay.) Too damn bad. You can't hurry l-o-v-e, and you can't hurry WOW (which emphatically does *not* mean you can't ease/urge/help them along).

* * *

Tom Wolfe's *A Man in Full* was the talk of many towns. First printing: a million copies. Wolfe first set the Big Novel in New York. Worked for *years* on it. Decided it was too similar to *Bonfire of the Vanities*. Scrapped the locale. Reset it in Atlanta. Began anew. And got to ... WOW! Y-e-a-r-s late/later.

T.T.D. / Slow Down!

1. Every Friday (or Saturday) morning revisit your one-page/single 5 x 7-inch card WOW description of the project: Are you still holding true to the dream? Perform this WOW-check religiously. Consider it renewing your vows. (WOW Vows? Gulp.)

2. Once a month (on long projects) review your project with your wackiest friend: Does it (still) pass her/his WOW Test? And/or: Meet with your teammates ... off site ... for a couple of hours ... and seriously consider scrapping/totally reconfiguring the project based on what you are learning. (Think Tom Wolfe.)

3. Conscientiously contribute a monthly project-progress report to the Divisional Newsletter ... mostly to see what you can say about the project that is new and WOW-worthy.

4. Religiously post a Friday p.m. **WOW-Mail** (e-mail) that details WOW-happenings/sightings for the week. If there aren't any ... worry ... a lot!

6.

It's elementary:

If you don't love "it," how can you expect others to?
Passion (yours) begets passion (theirs). Period.

> KEEP RETHINKING/
> REDEFINING/
> REFRAMING
> THE PROJECT UNTIL YOU . . .
> FALL IN LOVE.

The Nub

Commitment beats significance: This is not a frivolous suggestion. **There's solid evidence that the "importance" of a project is (far) less conclusive in determining its success than the level of commitment of its initiator(s).**

Never let yourself get sucked into a project you can't imagine falling in love with; you probably won't perform well. On the other hand, I've found that almost any project can be turned into an Object of Desire. For example, instead of tackling the whole project, chip off a piece of it that really challenges you/turns you on. Convert that piece into your immediate WOW-project-within-a-project: If that works out, move on to another bit that you can get worked up about. Once again, the trick is re-framing until the sparks fly.

(There's also a very strong message here for bosses: Shoving "important" projects down people's throats may well backfire. Make that:

WILL BACKFIRE.

Instead, either seek a project team leader who is genuinely turned on by the challenge—even if he/she is not your "best" person. Or redefine the project until it does attract the team leader you want.)

T.T.D./Love! (Or: Fergettaboutit)

1. Examine a prospective project closely. Deconstruct it into several sub-projects. Look for one or two of these that you find incredibly exciting/provocative/sexy. Make them your first projects-within-a-project.(Treat each bit as a b-i-g deal WOW Project in its own right.) Based on the results of these first sub-projects (Micro-WOWs), reframe the overall project so it provides the same turn-on.

2. Work with (prospective) teammates on project definition. **Don't rest until you have redefined the task/deliverables structure in a way that offers an immediately exciting—WOW!—challenge to *every* team member.**

3. Don't shy away from the term "love." Do you in fact l-o-v-e your project? **Measure it on a Love Scale:** 1 = Turnoff; 10 = Burning Desire. DO NOT PROCEED UNTIL YOUR—AND *EACH* OF YOUR TEAMMATES'— SCORE IS *AT LEAST* 7 OR 8.

7.

You—we all—"know beauty when we see it." So why not ... Beauty-in-Invoicing? (Or whatever the project topic is.) One thing's for sure: You'll never know until you ask!

The Nub

My goal (unabashed): reinvent thinking about projects. Add p-a-s-s-i-o-n. Learn to say/practice WOW ... love ... etc.

And ...

B - E - A - U - T - Y.

Why **(damn it!)** don't we use words/ideas like "beauty" in our daily project work? Why is beauty "not cool" between 9:00 a.m. and 5:00 p.m.? We know what beauty is. Right? So: Let's apply it to project formulation, project execution, and project deliverables. (Damn it.)

Consider these words from scientist David Gelernter in *Machine Beauty:*

> *The sense of beauty is a tuning fork in the brain that hums when we stumble on something beautiful....*

That art has entranced so many leading scientists is no accident.... They make no secret of beauty's central role in their work, yet we act as if we don't believe them. They talk about beauty, and we act as if they were kidding or humoring us.

When mathematical methods fail [in computer programming], the invariable response is, "Bring on more mathematical methods!" ... "The hell with mathematics, let's teach our programmers about beauty" is what we ought to hear.

Are you ready?

(I *know* you are *able*.)

Do you think **"it"** is important?

(Wouldn't you "love" to think back on a b-e-a-u-t-i-f-u-l project?)

T.T.D./B-e-a-u-t-y!

1. Find a good pal you deeply respect. (Maybe not a business associate.) Spend a dinner with her/him talking only about "beauty" ... *as it applies to work.* What *is* beauty? What are *examples* of beauty—in a restaurant meal, a hotel stay, a bank transaction, a gas pump, a hand tool, a form letter, a Web site? What is non-beauty/ugliness ... in a form, process, policy?

(BIG IDEA: Learn to *talk about* beauty ... in a natural/everyday way. E-v-e-r-y day.)

2. Look at your current project. Look at its short (one page or less) description. Examine its "deliverables." Are they—measure this, on a scale of 1 to 10—*beautiful*?

1 = Repulsive/Unfriendly.

5 = Personality-free.

10 = Breathtakingly Beautiful.

Not sure how to do the measurement? My advice: JUST DO IT. I.e., work with two or three colleagues, including a teammate and a customer: Talk about the project, its definition, its hoped-for results. Talk about beauty … in any realm of life. Then bring it (beauty) back to The Project. The discussion is likely to be messy/awkward, because this is unfamiliar turf. That's fine! (Good, in fact. Hey, we're trying to learn a whole new language.)

3. Renew the discussion of beauty-in-our-project on a weekly/monthly basis. Without fail.

4. Bring in cool outsiders to talk/work with your group. Architects. Dancers. Musicians. Etc.

* * *

The fairest thing we can experience is the mysterious. It is the fundamental emotion which stands at the cradle of true art and true science. He who knows it not and can no longer wonder, no longer feels amazement, is as good as dead, a snuffed-out candle.

—Albert Einstein

8.

Think: D-E-S-I-G-N.
Think: D-E-S-I-G-N-E-R-S. From the get-go.

Beauty/Grace
Friendliness/Identity/
WOW!/
Magical Moments =
It's a Designer's World!

(And ... yes ... I am talking about the warehouse or in-voicing project!) (Also see our forthcoming *50List ... the Design+Identity50.*)

The Nub

Put design at the *top* of the/your project team's list. And ... thus ... put design*ers* at the top.

Design—**beauty, grace, clarity + economy, user-friendliness**—is an idea that ... if factored in at all on the average project ... comes late. That is a dangerous ... foolish ... self-defeating ... approach. So ... stop!

61

Design is one of those magical realms that works on a subconscious level. It elevates us ... inspires us ... thrills us ... often without our understanding why. And: It is *the* essence of WOW. It is—oughta be!— a MAJOR component of *every* **(that's E-V-E-R-Y)** WOW Project!

Listen to what John Loring, design director of billion-dollar-grossing Tiffany & Co. has to say on the subject:

> *There is a gut, visceral reaction to design that works. If it has visual truth, you don't need to explain it. ... It is a terrible mistake to intellectualize design when it is, in fact, something physical. ...*
>
> *The Chicago Bulls are one of the great ballet-dance performances of our time. This is great modern imagery. You can't design for Tiffany & Co. if you didn't enjoy watching the Chicago Bulls play [during the Jordan years].... We don't like sweet and weak imagery at all; we like boldness... an aggressive stylishness and chic and elegance that is correct for modern times. We are not living in 18th-century France.*

Amen!

Big idea: **We are *all* designers.**

We—in accounting, HR, etc.—communicate to our internal/external customers and constituents via hundreds (literally) of design "cues" ... daily. The way our offices are laid out ... what hangs on the walls ... the shape, color, and size of every tool (in the broadest sense) we use ... our voice mail ... our Web site ... are all sending (clear ... if you are awake) design-driven messages.

And yet we rarely—if ever—think of ourselves as de-signers. **I AM UTTERLY DETERMINED TO CHANGE ALL THAT ...** *TO GET DESIGN/ DESIGNERS TO THE TOP OF ALL WOW PROJECT CREATORS' PRIORITY LISTS.*

Bottom-bottom line: Every project *can* be a WOW Pro-ject ... *can* be Way Cool ... *can* be Beautiful + Graceful. But ... not unless you take design very seriously ... ex-plicitly ... from the start.

T.T.D./Design Mindfulness

1. In the **next three days** have a two-hour meeting with your WOW Project Crew to discuss design. I.e.: HOW COULD DESIGN IMPACT US ... **REDEFINE OUR PROJECT** ... BECOME THE CENTERPIECE/ "IT"/SIGNATURE OF OUR PROJECT? (Please use my ... strong ... words ... or some close kin.)

2. Get a designer on board. Now!

3. Put design on **every** project meeting's agenda. (Preferably ... near/at the top.)

4. Consider going off on a day or two "design sensiti-zation course" ... of some sort.

5. Jot down in your journal ... every day ... at least *one* example of great design and *one* example of lousy design that you come across in your daily life. Remember, *every single* product you buy, check or document you sign, building or store you enter, and ad you read or watch was designed by somebody. How'd she/he do?

9.

The Nub

Our view: Every project *must* be evaluated— measured!—on a Revolutionary/WEIRD/Fit-for-the- Freaky-Times Scale. (Why: These *are* revolutionary times.)

How do you know if a project (and its deliverables) are "revolutionary"? Get weird/revolutionary users/custo- mers to evaluate it! Get the Coolest/Weirdest/Freakiest Dudes in your Rolodex to check it out! Get (very) youth- ful Internet-geek sorts to eyeball it! (*Every* project needs a major-Web angle. See No. 10 below.) Ask your 14-year- old daughter (son) what she (he) thinks. (Seriously!) And… as usual … the *real* key is getting comfortable with the word "revolutionary"; learn to use it in everyday-project conversation. The goal: to have the concept/imperative … of revolution … permeate the project's collective con- sciousness and (more important?) collective *sub*con- sciousness (after all, that's where most of WOW lives).

T.T.D./ Revolution!

1. Right now. No nonsense. **List *five* aspects of your project that are genuinely revolutionary.** (If you can't… reinvent/reframe.) (I'm dead serious.)

2. Invite **three freaks**—a freaky customer, a quirky academic researcher, a miscellaneous cool-freak person in your Rolodex—to evaluate the revolutionary aspects of your project. **ASAP.**

3. Have all team members write down the reasons why the project must be revolutionary … and what the word means to them. Hold a "revolutionary" meeting (hold it someplace weird—obviously) to discuss what everyone's written. The goal: to get the whole team on the same page … or, rather, off-the-page!

4. Have your teammates score—1 to 10—each of the project's deliverables on a Business-as-Usual to Revolutionary scale.

5. Put "revolutionary aspects" on the agenda of *every* Project Review Meeting.

Message:
GET EXPLICIT/TOP-OF-MIND AROUND THE WORD/ IDEA OF "REVOLUTIONARY."

10.

In a "Redefining" Way? (Big term ... but I'm serious.)
From the start?

The Nub

There is no such thing as a "revolutionary" (or even worth-getting-out-of-
bed-for) project ... if the Web doesn't
play a B-I-G/B-O-L-D role.

The project may be no more than the annual suppliers' "retreat." Well ... why not: (1) a special Web site for
the event? (2) Registration via the Web? (3) "Back home"
folks—not invited to the affair itself—plugged into
various presentations, live, via the Web? (4) Follow-up via
the Web? (Etc., Etc.)

T.T.D./Revolution = Welcome to
Web World!

1. Explicitly factor the Web into the project—any
project!— from conception. If you're mid-project, call a
special Web meeting.

TODAY.

2. Invite one or two local "Web gurus" to lunch to review your project plan and give you (bold-unflinching) Web input.

3. Have all team members regularly report on favorite Web addresses ... and assess their relevance to your project. (Be damn serious-systematic about this!)

4. Create your own ... **WOW Project Web site.** P.S.: The look and content of the site will communicate *a lot* about the project itself. No WOW Project would have a blah site. (Right? As in ... duh.)

11.

Amen. No, not every project is a Windows95. But every project should "make a noticeable difference." Even the "simple" redesign of a single form: "Does the b-e-a-u-t-y of the effort portend a whole new way of looking at things in our department? *Was It Worth Doing*?"

The Nub

I-M-P-A-C-T. Did the project change "the way we do business around here"? Did it matter/make a discernible difference? *W-H-O C-A-R-E-S?*

Ralph Waldo Emerson—the Self-Reliance Man—has returned to our midst as a modern-day hero: We must "stand for something"/"have a story to tell" in order to survive professionally. At the end of the day ... nobody ... not boss, not teammate, not technology ... can do it for you/me. Our fates ... and careers ... now more (*much more*) than ever ... rest in our own hands. This is one of the great truisms of our crazy, weird, wired, wonderful, revolutionary times.

The great majority of our waking hours are spent "doing" ... projects. So ... those projects are ... *our story*

... our professional legacy. **They are us.** Hence nothing(!)—*by definition*—is more important professionally than WAS IT [PROJECT] WORTH DOING?/DID IT [PROJECT] MATTER?

In short…our projects…*by definition*…must matter!

The bottom line, then, is clear: It is our Obligation No. 1—*to ourselves*—to make sure that *every* project—no matter how apparently mundane—is Worth Doing/Matters/Makes a Difference/Has Lasting I-m-p-a-c-t.

IMPACT, POLLOCK-STYLE

More WOW-ish criteria: While boning up for a visit to a Jackson Pollock retrospective at the Museum of Modern Art in New York in late 1998, I dug out Claude Cernuschi's book *Jackson Pollock*. In one chapter, the author focused on criteria critics use to evaluate an artist's career/work. To wit:

* *Fashion.* Was it "cool"?

* *Quality.* Was it great craft?

* *Originality.* Could it be classified as novel?

* *Influence. Was the path of the world of art altered significantly because of this person's work?*

Challenging list! So: **Apply it to your current project.** Now! (Okay?) (No baloney!) (And … no corner cutting. Use Cernuschi's terms. *Why not?*)

T.T.D./Was It Worth Doing?

1. Make a list of the two or three things you'd like to add to your résumé in the next 18 months to 2 years. Is your current project, as it is currently configured, on the list? (I.e., "does it matter"... BIG TIME... to *you*?) If not, reframe the project...**DRAMATICALLY**...or ease out of it.

2. Talk to a couple of wise folks (whom you admire) and ask them to *honestly* assess your current project:

DOES IT MATTER... OR DOES IT AMOUNT TO MARKING TIME?

(P.S.: To matter, a project does *not* have to be "big"; see No. 5 and No. 6 above re small projects that allow you to attack/perform end runs on problems of great significance.)

3. Beware mid-project slippage! *Vigilance!* **(Damn it!)** Keep the "Is It Worth Doing?" question alive throughout the project. Ask it (seriously + literally) at the end of every week... if not the end of every day.

11a.

MADE ANYBODY(S) ANGRY LATELY?

It's simple:
WOW Projects = Changing the rules.
Changing the rules = Pissing off members of the Establishment. (Period. I.e., It is axiomatic.)

The Nub

I'm not suggesting that you pick fights. But contention is part and parcel of a truly WOW/It-Matters project. Can you imagine the accomplishments of Martin Luther King, Jr.... with no enemies? Or Gandhi? Or: Franklin Roosevelt ... dealing with an isolationist Congress? (His 1941 Lend Lease deal with Churchill was clearly unconstitutional ... as were many of Lincoln's actions, 80 years earlier.)

Put another way: **Politics is life.** Including project life. And—perhaps paradoxically, or at least ironically— that goes double for "WOW Projects." That is, projects that—by definition—change the rules. You will, simply, have to deal with people who, for various reasons, don't want you to succeed: people who are envious, people who feel their turf is being invaded, people who have a b-i-g stake in the status quo, people who are just plain afraid of change. Therefore, you will need ... Herculean (or Clintonian) political skills to ... neutralize ... finesse ... and in some cases just plain outsmart-surround-coopt ... these naysayers. And, as usual, this notion of "project politics" is completely AWOL in "the literature" of project management.

T.T.D./Thicken Your Skin!

1. Think clearly about whom your project will annoy, anger, and/or agitate ... if it works as planned. (*All worthwhile-successful WOW Projects alter internal power relationships.*) In the early going, try to keep a low profile ... and avoid showing your full hand too early (i.e., when the project is particularly fragile). Develop powerful allies in those places that will benefit from your project. Map out (as in, study) very specifically who these prospective allies are and start to get them on board ... early. Modify elements of your project—i.e., add deliverables —to become even more attractive to those potential supporters-in-powerful-places.

2. Develop a precise plan for attracting/seducing your first key supporters.

Again, it's "politics." But remember: Politics = The Art of Getting Things Done.

No "politics" = No implementation.

And as to "the plan" ... political campaigns these days are hardly haphazard. Right? Couldn't you learn a thing or 2 or 22 from James Carville, one of the people to whom this book is dedicated?

12.

Our goal: to make our WOW Project Clients, starting with the first Alpha tester, no less than ... Raving Fans.

The Nub

WOW is *great*. (Hey ... that's the whole point of the exercise!) Beauty is *the* test of the project's lasting excellence. (Neglect beauty ... and you earn my open contempt!) Revolutionary is a *must*. (Revolutionary times ... **d e m a n d** revolutionary projects ... without doubt.) *Impact* is your calling card. (Long term, you must be able to respond positively to "Was It Worth Doing?")

So what's missing from our key attribute list? Answer: **THE C-L-I-E-N-T.** But if it's to be a WOW/Revolutionary/Beautiful/High-Impact/Worth-Doing Project ... is "Client inclusion" enough? My answer: No way! We want to meet the same "WOW-NOW-COME-HELL-*AND*-HIGH-WATER" standard with Clients that we demand from ourselves. Thence my advice: Steal shamelessly from Ken Blanchard and Sheldon Bowles. They wrote a best-selling book called *Raving Fans*. They begged us to go (far) beyond "customer satisfaction." To turn every customer-Client into a Hollywood-and-Vine billboard for our work ... i.e., a Raving Fan. So, I say:

Hold Yourself—**M E A S U R A B L Y !**— to the Client-as-Raving-Fan Standard.

Once more, it is—or may be—an opportunity for *more reframing*. Get a Seriously Cool Client—or two or three or four—on board early. (Very.) Have those Seriously Cool Clients co-design the project with you. Ask them, using this *precise* language:

"WHAT—PRECISELY, IN TERMS OF DELIVERABLES —CAN WE DO TO MAKE YOU A ... RAVING FAN?"

(Again: I beg you to use the Raving Fans words per se. And then to reframe the project as necessary to turn them into R.F.s.)

T.T.D./Raving Fans! (Or Bust!)

1. To begin with, think about—pretty precisely— what it means to be a "Raving Fan." What makes *you* a Raving Fan of a product or service? (And what turns you off? **Or leads you to be merely ... horror of horrors ... "satisfied" ... but emotionally *un*involved?**) Make a list of the stuff you *love* ... and *hate*. Then ask: Does our project include—*explicitly*—the sorts of things-hooks that I *love* as a user/Client? And does it explicitly exclude the things I *hate*? The idea: Start thinking about the **E**xplicit **R**aving **F**an **S**tandard.

2. Find *a* **(o n e !)** potential End User. Now. Walk her/him through the project. See if you get a Raving-Fan Reaction. (Not easy, since the project is so sketchy at this point.) At least engage her/him in a dialogue about Raving Fan-hood. Repeat this process as you reframe/refine the project definition.

3. Study/research—carefully!—Client reactions to the current version of, say, the Business Process that your project aims to WOW-ify. Do you have a deep understanding of users ... today? What they "love"/"hate"/merely "like"?

What **makes them irate**? What **thrills them**? You must ... **know this** ... if you want to turn them into Raving Fans of the revolutionized process ... tomorrow. Hint: Look for dissatisfied users as your first guinea pigs. The "average" user may be too indifferent—e.g., only vaguely annoyed with the way things are. You want a firebrand user who is **pissed off** ... at you ... **today** ... and becomes a fan (of the raving sort) tomorrow. Win that ornery soul over ... and think how blissed out the average user will be!

12a.

WOMEN-AS-RAVING FANS. WOMEN TAKE TO PRODUCTS/SERVICES— AND, THENCE, "PROJECT DELIVERABLES"—FOR (VERY) DIFFERENT REASONS THAN MEN.

The Nub

American women are Earth's Biggest Economy. (Responsible, among other things, for $4.8 trillion of the U.S. GDP.) Businesses owned by American women—there are more than nine *million*—bring in more revenue ($3.6 trillion) than the GDP of the entire German economy. Yet women are mis-/under-/poorly-served by virtually all large health care providers ... financial services companies ... auto makers (and, God knows, auto dealers!) ... computer makers ... etc. (I could say much more ... and *will* in the forthcoming companion to this book, *the Women's Market50*.)

Concerning WOW Projects, however, my message is short and ... I hope ... sweet:

IF WOMEN—AS RETAIL OR BUSINESS-TO-BUSINESS CONSUMERS—ARE YOUR TARGET ... ACT ACCORDINGLY! (And—more or less—they oughta be your target.)

That is, *every* aspect of project/ product design and delivery must explicitly reflect women-as-target-user.

Address this up front ... not as an afterthought.

CONSISTENT EVIDENCE

The evidence is bizarrely consistent. Financial services. Health services. Computer systems. Autos. You name it. "Guys" are "interested in getting through the transaction"; women are interested in "the relationship" with the provider. Women by and large don't want an in-your-face, high-pressure sales pitch; they want to study the offering and respond in a measured fashion. (E.g.: See "FemaleThink," in Faith Popcorn's *Clicking*.)

**These e-x-a-c-t same ideas carry forward
to internal customers for a business-process
redesign project.** E.g.: Are you just "selling" new fea-
tures? Or are you selling a new, more thoughtful approach to unit-to-unit relationships?

T.T.D./Women-as-Project-Users

**1. Are women—internal or external Clients
—principal users of this project's deliverables? Could they be?** (Are you perfectly sure
about your answer to this question?)

2. Is women-as-primary-users *explicitly* factored into
every element of project design and execution? Can you
reframe the project for women-as-users?

3. Are you staffed—advisors, Clients/potential Raving Fans—with the right people to help you reframe (and
execute!) this project with women-as-users in mind?
Hint (duh!?): This means having women on board...
in unmistakable leadership roles.

4. IS THIS—WOMEN-AS-USERS—A BIG

$$(WOW+!)$$

DEAL TO YOUR TEAM/DESIGN PROCESS?

If not... why not? (Think about it. Talk about it. Explicitly. Regularly.)

13.

PIRATES-ON-THE-HIGH-SEAS.
"WE" ARE ON A MISSION/
CRUSADE. WE PLAN TO UPSET
THE APPLECART (CONVENTIONAL
WISDOM) BIG TIME . . . AND
MAKE A DAMN DIFFERENCE.

We are Pilgrims . . .

Pioneers . . .

Pirates.

And we are about to embark upon . . . an Adventure.

(And: Please *do* capitalize that "A" in Adventure!)

The Nub

Piracy. Pioneering. Flipping-smashing-bashing apple-carts. **A**dventure! The point:

YOU'LL NEVER MAKE A DIFFERENCE UNLESS YOU PURPOSEFULLY CONCOCT (AND EXECUTE) A "MEMORABLE ADVENTURE."

During the development of the first Mac, Steve Jobs flew a pirate flag above his development center at Apple. (He was pulling an end run—of epic proportions—on his own company!)

The idea here is practical: We won't make (historic) headway against the status quo ... unless we can convince our fellow pirates/shipmates (users, suppliers, direct teammates) that we are all on a **V**oyage—*an* **A**dventure—worth signing up for.

Webster's defines the word "adventure" as "a daring undertaking; an unusual, stirring, often romantic experience." I love that! "Often romantic": When was the last time—precisely—you thought of your project/job as ...

r - o - m - a - n - t - i - c ?

It can/should/will be ... **if** you consider/follow the actions in this book. (We think.) This *is* what it's all about. Making your project/life ... daring ... stirring ... **romantic** ... an **A**dventure.

PROJECT-AS-NARRATIVE

A WOW Project is an unfolding narrative ... a story ... a good yarn. In our selected resources (end of the book) you'll find no traditional project management texts. Instead, you'll discover Great Yarns: The development of radar in World War II. The creation of the Boeing 747. The invention of a pioneering computer at Data General.

These are ... Projects Worth Doing ... Work that Matters. As project chief you are creating a narrative, a story, a good yarn. If you look at the process-journey that way, you and your gang will have a lot more fun and, I'll wager, dramatically up the odds of a WOW Outcome!

* * *

WHAT A WASTE: A LIFE THAT'S NOT AN ADVENTURE.
OR, AT LEAST, AN ATTEMPT TO BE AN ADVENTURE.

T.T.D./Adventure! Piracy!

1. So ... *is* this (our prospective WOW Project) a
g-e-n-u-i-n-e **A**dventure? Why? As in: Why should *I* sign
up to stick my neck out and take (a lot of) flak? What
exactly makes it worth the risk? What makes it daring,
unusual, stirring ... *r-o-m-a-n-t-i-c*?

2. Use the/my terms: Adventure ... Piracy ... Episode-
on-the-High-Seas ... Romantic. Once more: Words *do* matter. (A lot.) And: *Hot* words beget *hot* projects/*hot*
co-conspirators/*hot* sponsors/*hot* users.

3. Start ... now ... a *Log of the Voyage to [Your WOW Project Name]*. Adopt all aspects of the Adventure idea. (Perhaps read collectively the books about the
Arctic-Antarctic explorers as inspiration. Peary. Scott.
Shackleton. Amundsen.)

14.

And you:

The WOW Project benefits immensely from cachet—and a sanctuary/lair/ privacy.

"A place" could equal the corner table in the brew pub where you meet on Thursday evenings ... or an unused 10 x 12-foot office where you start hanging out and creating your nest. Eventually "the place" should become a vibrant nerve center/War Room, not unlike the White House Map Room.

The Nub

Seems an odd entry on this list, eh? I don't think so. **WOW Projects are all about ... character ... fortitude ... insouciance ... panache. So our WOW-pirate gang needs ... a pirates' lair.**

History is on my side here: Most conspiracies—and what is a WOW Project if not a conspiracy?—have been hatched at corner tables in favorite pubs or in converted warehouses or garret apartments. Someplace where a band of passionate outlaws can let their hair down...debate ideas...spin dreams...make plans...devise, revise, analyze...recharge their faith. So our giddy adventurers need a "joint" of some sort or other to call their piratical own. Later, the "space"/"studio"/"sanctuary" becomes the more formal—if frenzied—hatchery from which secretive-yet-cool-stuff is seen to emanate.

Another space/place advantage: It helps build buzz! Folks start asking, "What is this band of merry men and women up to? The energy and excitement oozing from that dingy little room is palpable, awesome!" Curiosity and expectation build, colleagues want to climb on board, and your WOW Project is—like all "places"—suddenly very much on the map.

T.T.D./"Hangout" Power!

1. Scrounge a little space—preferably crummy—to turn into a team/co-conspirators meeting room. Fit it out comfortably (*never* formally). Pepper the walls with draft mission statements, rough timelines, posters of heroes, snapshots of milestones, celebrations, follies, etc.

2. Okay, it *is* spin doctoring, but consciously work on ...*cachet.* Make "the space"/studio a bit mysterious and even kinky. WOW Projects = Beneficiaries of Buzz. So ... work on that buzz/spin...assiduously.

15.

That's what the sports psychologists urge us to do. Why not the same with your current project? Write up the outcome of your current project as an entry in your updated, year-end, 2000 résumé.

Does it sing to you? If not... more reframing is in the cards.

The Nub

WOW Project = WOW Pictures. From the get-go. I-m-a-g-i-n-e! V-i-s-u-a-l-i-z-e! Paint the picture in your mind of the finished project! Among other things: Paint/Visualize = *More* encouragement for Design Mindfulness. Right? (Revisit No. 7, No. 8 above.)

T.T.D./Pictures that Stir the Soul!

1. R-I-G-H-T N-O-W. HAVE EVERY INITIAL PROJECT CO-CONSPIRATOR WRITE UP THE FINISHED VERSION OF YOUR WOW PROJECT ... FOR HIS/HER YEAR-END RÉSUMÉ. COMPARE NOTES. (SWAP DREAMS!) IF YOU'RE NOT "AWED" BY WHAT YOU COME UP WITH ... REFRAME THE PROJECT. (NO MATTER WHERE—HOW FAR ALONG—IT STANDS.)

16.

Creative stuff comes from creative teams aiming to serve a creative, crazy-quilt mix of customers/Clients. R-I-G-H-T?

Walk around *any* vital American city. Guess what? You'll see people of all colors, backgrounds, ethnicities, eccentricities, genders, shapes, etc.

Hooray for it! We're entering the Global Century, and we are the Global Nation—still a Mecca of Opportunity, a roiling pot of exuberance! Of enterprise! Of excitement!

Diversity = Range of Perspectives = Effectiveness = Probability of WOW!

So: *DOES your initial band of pirates encompass an **E**xuberant **M**ess of **B**ackgrounds?* And: Are you *explicitly* factoring in rainbow-of-*users* from the start?

The Nub

This is the ultimate no-brainer (or ought to be): Your project is as cool as the cool-ness of those involved! Limit yourself to middle-aged white males and you are ... doomed ... **d-o-o-m-e-d by d-e-f-i-n-i-t-i-o-n** ... to anti-WOW-ness!

I *am* a diversity freak.(But there's not a dollop of "P.C." in it/me. P.C. is about sanctimonious, self-righteous, tread-lightly-because-you-might-offend behavior. WOW … and the diversity *necessary* to achieve WOW … is about unpretentious, offend-the-powers-that-be, in-your-face, c-o-o-l behavior.)

* * *

WOW = Diversity = Wild Mix = Cool = F-R-E-A-K-S. Period.

* * *

I can state this unequivocally: The best (WOW-est) projects I've been around/on/in have benefitted from a pride of misfits/diverse folks who brought an extraordinary "diversity" of views/backgrounds/lifestyles/talents to bear.

You heard it here first: Young is different from old. Women are different from men. African Americans are different from Caucasians who are different from Asian Americans. Gay is different from straight. Etc. You will not —pure and simple—create a WOW Project from a homogeneous team. Period.

T.T.D./Rainbow Moment!

1. So… **IS YOUR PROJECT TEAM A RAINBOW?** (Talk about this with teammates. Now.)

2. What are you doing to make your WOW Project Team a rainbow (color/age/education/gender/race/etc.)?

3. Talk to three interesting close associates: Get their recommendations for Rainbow Additions to your incipient WOW Project Team. **ASAP.**

4. Extend the Rainbow Idea to … Clients, suppliers, advisors … anyone, that is, involved with the project.

* * *

IF YOUR PROJECT TEAM IS HOMOGENEOUS YOU ARE CONSIGNED TO WOW-LESS-NESS!

17.

PERT charts—etc.—are fine. But the real "planning" answer for a WOW Project is a no-baloney "small-business plan." *A project—any WOW Project—is a small/micro-business.* So: The project plan/proposal ought to read/smell like a small-business plan.

The Nub

A Cool/Rockin'/WOW Project is ... in many (essential) ways ... a self-contained "small business." **A WOW Project is a quintessential startup.** The "plan" for it should therefore—by definition—be a no-nonsense *business plan.*

T.T.D./Business Plan

1. Plan? *Damn right!* **But does your WOW Project Plan have the pragmatism, the drive, the hard deadlines, and hard deliverables of a hungry startup's formal business plan?**

2. Gather a dozen first-rate business plans—from venture capitalists, pals, etc. Compare your project plan to their plans. Does it measure up? If not ... regroup, rethink, *reframe.* (*I.e.: Imagine you are going to a venture capitalist for first-round funding: Will your WOW Project Plan entice him/her to part with his/her money?*)

18.

**THINK/OBSESS . . .
D - E - A - D - L - I - N - E.
BE RIDICULOUSLY/ABSURDLY/
INSANELY DEMANDING OF
YOURSELF/YOUR LITTLE BAND
OF RENEGADES.**

Think "six months" ... and sure 'nuf, it'll take six+ months. Think "five days" ... and I'll bet you'll get something serious done in five days. (Or three!) WOW Projects: "Dreams with deadlines," per Great Groups guru Warren Bennis.

The Nub

Do it ... **N O W.** I/we'll have lots more to say about this. (See the section on Implementation.) But the main idea: There's no room for procrastination/dawdling in the pursuit of big "dreams." To the contrary, the lordliest "dreamers" I've met also topped the Pragmatism Scale: They are determined to conduct *real* tests and corner *real* customers ... *ASAP.* You make your bones in the WOW Project Business not by spinning tall tales but by *doing* cool stuff ... *right now.*

Momentum is the **Big Enchilada** in politics/projects/life/just-about-everything. It's that forward force, that drive, that energy surge that creates a tidal wave of inevitability around WOW! Lose momentum and you're a deflated balloon ... limp and listless ... and decidedly uninspiring. Maintain it ... and you've upped the odds significantly in your favor.

Momentum is a fragile force. **Its worst enemy: p-r-o-c-r-a-s-t-i-n-a-t-i-o-n.** Its best friend: a deadline (think Election Day). Implication No. 1 (and there is no No. 2): Get to work! NOW!

T.T.D./Deadline City!

1. You "love" it. It's "cool." GREAT! But: Concoct a *real* test of some part of "it" in the next ... 72 *hours*.

MANTRA: MAKE IT REAL ... N-O-W.

("But isn't 72 hours unrealistic?" a colleague asked. "No way," I replied. "The true 'fast prototypers' tell me ... 'No. No. No.'" I.e.: You can make a "little" "real" test of s-o-m-e-t-h-i-n-g that quickly ... **if** you are determined.)

2. Constantly talk (and live): *real* ... *now* ... *test* ... *deadline.* Never let our lovely "it" (WOW Project) become chimerical.

3. Set practical deadlines ... today! (The first of which should be no more than **f-i-v-e days** from now.) (No kidding.)

4. Post deadlines. Prominently. Publicly. In the Team Room. Quarto size. Team members shouldn't be able to go far without tripping over ... **d-e-a-d-l-i-n-e-s.**

19.

You need some**one** to talk to/vent with.
Find a wise and sympathetic elder if
you can.

Use her (him) as an occasional sounding board/inter-
ference runner. Hint: This is surprisingly important!

The Nub

Projects *are* a team sport. But WOW Projects can—
ironically—be lonely. Why? Because the WOW Project
aims to tip-flip-batter more than a couple of applecarts.
Hence, the established apple vendors are going to lob
(vitriolic) potshots your way. (This is especially galling...
given your true believer's "knowledge" that this is the
greatest, most righteous project ever.) One big answer:
a pal. It can be a spouse, of course. But I also urge a "wise
advisor"... or mentor... from work. He can talk you down
from your anger... talk you up after setbacks... and offer
sage advice on how to handle that thorny little (big?)
problem (such as that recently minted MBA analyst determined to make your life miserable and squeeze every

ounce of WOW-ness out of your project). If at all possible, you and your mentor should schedule a weekly phone call ... a biweekly or monthly lunch ... even if things are apparently going smoothly. Freud revolutionized human relations with his passion for "the talking cure." Think of this as your WOW Project's "talking preventive medicine."

In my big project at McKinsey & Co., I would have gone 'round the bend without a couple of wise sounding boards to vent on and be calmed down by. At points—my case—these folks ran interference for me and smoothed Important Feathers I had ruffled.

T.T.D./Wise Advisor-Shrink

1. Take this seriously! *You* **cannot** *go it alone!* (Trust me. **Please.**) Schedule a lunch—in the next week—with, say, a former boss to talk about your project and how she could help mentor you through the perils that lie ahead. Do not rest until you have, in effect, signed up such an advisor. (If there's no one close at hand, go farther afield. But ... do it!) (And show your appreciation in ways large and small.)

2. Ask your advisor, above all, to shoot straight with you: **to warn you when you've gone over the edge** ... to tell you when you're being a jerk ... to alert you when you're chasing down a blind alley, at 90 m.p.h., heading straight for a brick/career-ending wall.

3. Religiously schedule a call/lunch/after-work session with your advisor. **Keep her plugged into project goings-on** ... even though she is not in the official chain of command.

20.

Take a would-be co-conspirator to lunch … once a week.

Sales starts on Day No. 1: So start networking with sympathizers/freaks … now.

The Nub

Sure, we're talking about "creating" and "reframing" the project in this first of four sections. And, sure, it's *your* fire in *your* belly that rules. Still, the time to go beyond solo is … **NOW.**

The wise advisor (see No. 19 above) is your sounding board. But WOW Projects are mostly a *sales* discipline (see more below). And you need—desperately *and* from the get-go!—enthusiastic allies. Eventually you'll have to build a rich network of supporters. But just the act of earning the first couple of allies will help you shape and sharpen your WOW Project Selling Skills. You'll become a more articulate, passionate advocate for Your Baby.

Fact is, *all* (early) supporters are mostly created equal. You need supporters. Period. Not a "famous" supporter … but **a** supporter. Any Damn Supporter.

TRUTH BE TOLD, THERE IS SOMETHING (GREAT) TO SAY FOR THE RELATIVELY POWERLESS EARLY SUPPORTER: HE/SHE SIGNS ON SOLELY BECAUSE OF HIS/HER PASSION FOR THE PROJECT.

The "passion aura"—and the ability to recruit even one passionate ally—is what matters at first.

So quit busting your pick ... trying to sign up the "big woman/man." Work to attract people who c-a-r-e. Look for quirky, caring, driven, oddball types and turn them into associate members of your one- (two-? three-?) man/woman band. **ASAP.**

T.T.D./ First, **Dear** Co-conspirator(s)

1. Identify *two* pals to talk to about the project ... in the next week. Set up a breakfast/ lunch meeting with each of them. Lay out your aspirations. Let them kibitz. See if they'll tentatively sign on. Goal: Another meeting! (No more ... no less.)

2. Brainstorm with that first supporter about a list of targets ... folks, mostly *unempowered,* who might like to get involved. Put together a pretty concrete schedule for contacting, say, five to ten people.

3. Start a Master File, a Formal Contact List, which tracks, as a determined salesman would (that's what you are ... right?), the people you want to involve—in *any* way —in your project. Keep the List current as Hell! Carry it with you! *Obsess on it!*

4. Never—ever!—let an opportunity pass to brief a

would-be pirate/co-conspirator. You are in the briefing business. Period. (Just ask Peter Ueberroth—head of the 1984 L.A. Olympics—or any other project fanatic.)

YOUR MANTRA: I LIVE TO BRIEF!

20a.

FIND AT LEAST ONE USER/CO-CONSPIRATOR. NOW. THINK USER FROM THE START.

"Customers"/*a* customer/a *freaky* customer's view and counsel is integral/imperative ... from the outset!

The Nub

Again: We are "just" formulating the project. But ... it's never too early to recruit your first "real" user.

No! No! No! My language is w-r-o-n-g. Forget "never too early." Instead: **It's soon too late to enlist the first real-user/co-conspirator!** Not "a" user. But a *pirate*-user. That is, a genuine enthusiast. Satisfy, delight, *thrill* that pirate-user and you'll know you're on the right track. And ... off to the Raving Fan Races described above.

The power/payoff: (1) instant credibility—*one* "real" customer/person/user believes in "it"; (2) a practical litmus-person-outsider to test the "it" with which you are already in love; (3) the start of a genuine, broad Community-of-Fervent-Supporters. *(P.S.: This applies e-x-a-c-t-l-y as much to internal business-form redesign as it does to a new version of a $50,000 automobile.) (Bonus: A supplier/pirate/co-conspirator is a fabulous early addition to the team, too.)*

Such folks help your sales job ... buttress your credibility ... *and* make-the-damn-project-better-*and*-more-real-*and*-more-WOW.

T.T.D./User-Partner No. 1

1. Who *is* your project "for"? Conjure up three or four quintessential first/brave/pioneering users. Call them! Take them to lunch! Lay out your dream! Try to enlist them ... **for something** ... no matter how small (e.g., host a meeting—three folks—for other possible prospective users).

2. Now get *real* "real." Sign the user up for a test of the first partial prototype. And, though you've got little concrete going, schedule the prototype test ... NOW. (It is *never* too early to go "real" ... as long as the user is a sympathizer.)

3. Put the user/co-conspirator in "official" charge of finding/signing up fellow user-pioneers. Give him/her an early stake in the project's payoff.

4. Start a formal Users Council (Raving Fans Club) ... N-O-W. (Again: It's never too early—but it's soon too late!)

21.

CONSIDER CARRYING AROUND
A LITTLE CARD THAT READS:

WOW!
BEAUTIFUL!
REVOLUTIONARY!
IMPACT!
RAVING FANS!

And on your wall: Pin a large sheet of butcher paper on which you describe WOW!/Beautiful!/Revolutionary!/ High Impact!/Raving Fans! outcomes for your current project. (Or something of the sort.)

The Nub

This may be "the" big idea of this book. (And your life!?)

(Big Words.) We urge—*beg!*—you to **explicitly m-e-a-s-u-r-e/q-u-a-n-t-i-t-a-t-i-v-e-l-y against** our BIG FIVE: WOW!/Beautiful!/Revolutionary!/ Impact!/Raving Fans! The contentions:

(1) If you can't explicitly *aspire* to such measures ... you can't possibly pull off WOW (and the other four).

(2) You must think ... M-E-A-S-U-R-E-M-E-N-T. **We all know what these words/terms mean.**

Therefore, they are/can be a universal language your team can use to determine and grade its status: "This is a '7' on the **B**eautiful **P**rojects **S**cale. We're moving in the right direction." Or: "This is a '3' with **T**argeted **R**aving **F**ans. It's time to reframe this project, we're off track." (P.S.: Our research says people will closely agree on the scores for all five dimensions, once they've gotten used to talking about these ideas.)

(3) You should **(m u s t!)** keep this set of ideas/criteria … constantly … in-your-collective-faces. Hence, the little card … and the butcher paper on the wall in the team space.

As one of my friends said of her pet passion-project: *"I want this project to be so cool, so much in defiance of 'conventional wisdom,' that it makes me giggle. I remind myself of that a half dozen times a day."*

Amen! (Should I add **G**iggle **S**cale to the criteria set above?) (I'm tempted.)

* * *

It boils down to "Living-the-WOW-Life."

MY OWN MANTRA: LIFE IS TOO SHORT FOR NON-WOW PROJECTS!

* * *

I'm not pushing "my" five words/phrases to the exclusion of all others. They just happen to be ones that work for me … and I've now seen them work for countless others. But I am pushing s-o-m-e-t-h-i-n-g. Nintendo's chief said to one of his game designers, **"Make something great."** ("Great" is a great word!) David Ogilvy, the premier ad man, ordered a colleague to create an **"immortal"** ad for children's clothing made of viyella, a British blend of cotton and wool. ("Immortal" is another terrific—stretch!—word.) Speaking of immortal: The immortal dance producer Sergei Diaghilev said to one of his dancers, **"Amaze me."** (Three loud cheers for "amazing" as a project criterion!) *Wallpaper* magazine cited a grocery store for a major design award: **"This new store rocks."** ("This project rocks" gets my nod of distinct approval!) So pick your own wild/woolly/stretch/cool/rockin' criteria. Okay?

T.T.D./ Measure Against the Big Five!

1. Discuss with your project-mates the five "big" words/terms: WOW!/Beautiful!/Revolutionary!/Raving Fan!/Impact! Are they right for you? (If not ... choose your own BIG FIVE ... but make sure *each* word/term is Grand-Bold! That is: See above.) Discuss at length your list and what each word/term means.

2. Measure your reframed project(s) against your a-w-e-s-o-m-e criteria. Now! (And: Repeatedly.)

3. Make that card—**Draft No. 1, right now**—with the WOW!/Impact!/etc. desired outcomes for the current project. Spend *lots* of time with your colleagues on the exact wording. (And ... redux ... revisit ... regularly.)

REPRISE: CREATE!

The Project50 = 50 items. (Plus a little cheating.) And I've just spent 42 percent of my coin (21/50) on the "warm-up" ... *inventing* a WOW Project. Seems excessive, right?

I don't think so. I admit that *I* was surprised at first that "inventing" merited almost half the "stuff." But then it occurred to me that this-is-the-whole-bloody-point! This—creating WOW**!**—is precisely what we ignore in most discourses on project management. In fact, how many such discourses have *anything* on project creation? (Let alone "beauty.") It—creation—is a "given" in traditional coverage of the topic.

My take: to the contrary! The "inventing" of the WOW Project is its most important element. It's crucial to build WOW into the foundation of a project ... (beautiful) brick by (cool, freaky, fabulous) brick. Trying to force WOW into a project that started life as Blah or Okay or Pretty Good is a whole Hell of a lot harder than fending off Blah/Okay/Pretty Good from a project with a firm WOW Footing. I hope—by now—that you're on board with that idea. Or, at least, intrigued by it.

* * *

The genesis of my last book, *The Circle of Innovation*: We are trapped in a sea of sameness—at exactly the wrong moment. Quality is generally up. Great! But you can't tell one product/service from another. My point, in part, here: "Sameness" in products and services spouts from companies where most work, most projects end up being "mediocre successes."

* * *

I do have a loud voice. But I'm actually a pretty conservative guy. So even I was surprised—at me—when I found, at a recent seminar, that I'd jumped up on a chair. (Never done that before.) "How many of you are in IS?" I shouted. (Many hands went up.) "Well," I continued my rant, "there's a special ring in Dante's Hell for IS people who don't do WOW in 1999. You are the keepers of the tools of this incredible revolution. If you choose to use them in a non-revolutionary way, a non-WOW way ... then you have betrayed the faith."

Okay, it *was* a little over the top. But I said it with a friendly grin. The point here:

THIS IS THE HOUR FOR WOW PROJECTS. PERIOD.

And it starts at the start: the creation phase.

Now ... on to the next missing link ...

II. sell!

"Damn few" is the answer. (None?) And therein lies the problem. WOW Projects *must* be sold ... to team members, higher-ups, freaky first-users, and ultimately customers-at-large. Learning to **s-e-l-l** is a hefty part of the battle; it forces clarity, focus, drive, faith.

Look at a real-world WOW Project. For three lonely, passionate, civic-minded zealots determined to add an after-school Teen Room to the town's Rec Center, the "timeline" and all the other project management "musts" are the least of it. The most of it: **infecting others with their zeal.** And, eventually, getting the whole community behind them to the tune, among other things, of $250,000. It's pure sales ... just like Willy Loman ... or your insurance agent ... or peddling Girl Scout cookies or cosmetics for one of my all-time heroes, Mary Kay.

Well...**your WOW Project is that Teen Room.**
Can you ignore timelines and all the other management
basics? Of course not! But without a sterling sales job
(*and* the WOW/Beauty/Impact to back it up)...the timeline ain't going to do you much/a-n-y good!

* * *

**What set Edison apart was that, with all his boundless
exaggeration, he conveyed the feeling that he would
succeed. No matter what the obstacles, he would pound
away until they were demolished.**
— Robert Conot, biographer

A really new idea has at first only *one* believer.
— John Masters, co-founder,
Canadian Hunter Exploration, Ltd.

**Whenever anything is ... being done, I have learned, it is
being done by a monomaniac with a mission.**
— Peter Drucker

* * *

*Sir Ernest Shackleton. Antarctic explorer. Greatest
leader ever, according to some. Robert Falcon Scott. Antarctic explorer. Brave beyond measure. Sir Ranulph Fiennes.
Modern man. First successful transpolar adventurer. WHAT
A GROUP! (And talk about WOW Projects!) Ever read books
about them? If you have, you'll know one (other) thing: Reluctantly or not, each was/became a great salesman. Even
a bit of a flim-flam man. Both Scott and Shackleton, for example, were late joining their defining voyages. Why? They
were still at home in England ... making sales (money-
raising) calls!* **(Think about it.)**

22.

And on one 5 x 7-inch index card.

Selling = Brevity. And clarity.

Project Champion to would-be supporter: "Can I have three [*two! one!*] minute/s of your time?" Because ... believe it... in today's overbooked world, that's all you're going to get.

So ... BOIL IT DOWN ... to a brilliant/WOW/brief/world-class sales and positioning pitch.

The Nub

It's ... sales ... stupid! I've got a lot of (big) problems with the normal approach to project management: E.g., where's the WOW/Beauty/etc.? But perhaps my biggest hang-up is the failure to see the project conceptualization-to-execution-to-pass-off process as what it quintessentially is:

Namely ... a pure S-A-L-E-S GAME!

To wit:

<u>Sales</u> = G-r-a-b-b-i-n-g the attention of would-be supporters.

<u>Sales</u> = Showing early/practical progress.

<u>Sales</u> = A COMPELLING STORY.

In the movie *Amistad,* John Quincy Adams (played by Anthony Hopkins) counsels with slave-turned-abolitionist-lawyer Theodore Joadson (played by Morgan Freeman): "Early in my career in the law I learned that whoever has the best story wins. So what's your story?"

Let's take that love of yours...the would-be WOW Project that you hope to be bragging about five (ten?!) years from now. And get our "story"/"pitch" right. Which means, first and foremost, boiling it down. **And, then, boiling it down again.** Remember, even though that door of opportunity may be open, it can slam shut at any second. People are busy with their own lives and if you don't hook 'em ... **QUICKLY** ... you're finished. (At least, for the moment.)

In our WOW Projects seminars, "Honing the pitch" is our premier exercise ... and the one participant/customers tell us is *the* most valuable.

Honing the pitch: At 7:25 a.m. you enter the elevator in the 60-story tower you call (professional) home. The Group Executive—her very self!—enters after you. And ... the doors close. *You've got her—all to yourself—for, say, at least 35 floors.* And you're in love ... with your project! So ... you've got, say, two(!!) minutes "to sell."

And/so:
WHAT'S YOUR **COMPELLING** STORY?

T.T.D./ The Elevator Spiel!

1. Create a one-page (max!) description of your project.

2. Boil the one page down to five "bullet points" that fit on a (*one*... literally) 5 x 7-inch index card.

3. Prepare—**and rehearse the daylights out of!**—your two-minute "elevator spiel." Try it out on a buddy. Try it out on your spouse. Try it out on a cabby.

4. Refine "the pitch"—the 5 x 7-inch card, the spiel—constantly. With graphic designers. With speech coaches. I.e., take it s-e-r-i-o-u-s-l-y.

* * *

WHAT **IS** YOUR STORY?

22a.

The "pitch"—and every aspect of the project—works best if there is a compelling theme/image/hook that makes the whole thing cohere, resonate, and vibrate with life.

That is: Provocative, powerful, indelible metaphor = Ultimate in WOW Communication. Hint: This is worth days of your precious time!

The Nub

Sales is grubby. Sales is getting doors slammed in your face. So... why this bit on metaphors (the ultimate abstraction)? Answer: A compelling metaphor is the "story" (see above) distilled—enhanced!—to a picture/image/five-words-or-less. *(Think of it as the WOW Project's bumper sticker!)*

I've worked on a handful of important projects. And at some point it dawned on me (hey, I'm not an "ad guy") that a succinct... from the heart... metaphor/picture is worth far more than a thousand words.

Once I figured this out I became a possessed fanatic. I now *demand* (to the limited extent that I can) that any project team I'm working with spend a bucket of time on "the metaphor."

Are we the equivalent of "Just do it"? Or "We try harder"? Or … a band of pirates? Or … two star-crossed lovers on the prow of an enormous ship? (*Titanic* was a serious WOW Project!) Or … Renegades on the Move? Or … or …??

You may not come up with the "perfect picture"—not even the big ad agencies do it with any regularity. But merely searching for the right picture/image/metaphor is a significant step forward. It concentrates the mind. It enhances the sales focus. It injects the liveliness of imagery into your/your team's routine thinking.

So … trust me and at least try!

T.T.D./ Metaphor-Picture Power!

1. So, try (by yourself, for starters) reducing your project to a metaphor/picture: "Seductive invoices," "Sick-leave policy that says 'We care,'" "Partners-in-purchasing." Whatever. (Those are all pretty lame. You *can* do lots better than that. Right?) (Hint: We spent *months* coming up with the **!** as symbol for our "anti-Dilbert Movement." See page 202.)

2. Work on your awareness: Collect metaphors! Over the course of the next few weeks, tear out and file several dozen newspaper/magazine ads that have terrific slogans or images. Put them in a file folder. When the time comes to work with your team on the image/metaphor/

picture for your project, use these ads (etc.) as thought-starters. Perhaps bring in a copy writer from a local ad agency, on a day's consultancy fee, to work with you on this. (This doesn't have to be a jillion-dollar fee paid to Planet's Best. Any sizeable town includes at least a handful of tiny, creative agencies.)

3. Shop—with total openness!—your metaphor/picture to all sorts of people … in the next three days. (One indicator of the power of the picture/image/metaphor idea: *Everyone* has, I've learned, an opinion … which means that you have c-o-n-n-e-c-t-e-d … which is the whole point!)

4. Schedule a "metaphor meeting" in the next 10 days—with all prominent parties-to-the-project present. Work—for a full day, if necessary—on that image, slogan, picture, metaphor. **(And nothing else.)**

5. *Do not rest!* Re-visit the image/picture/metaphor every few weeks! Don't be afraid to fine tune/completely toss out your metaphor. Your project is a WOW-in-Progress. The last thing you need is a metaphor frozen in stone. Engage more (and more!) (*and* more!) people in the quest-for-the-perfect-metaphor. To wit:

This **is** you!
This **is** the quintessential expression of your project's character!
This *is* the ultimate distillation/sales pitch.

23.

No. 22 above focuses on selling the big cheese. Important. But perhaps not even "sales" priority No.1.

The Nub

Sales—and the measure of the effectiveness of the two-minute spiel—is initially about your ability to fire up early supporters. Therefore *The Pitch* must be aimed at peers, primarily, not honchos. Fact is, it's probably going to be a while before you get to the chairwoman (or even want to get to her).

One of the biggest mistakes fired-up project champions can make is going "up" too early.

The better idea is to take our hot idea ... **see if we can sell it to a-n-y-o-n-e** ... test it ... and test it again ... honing it every time ... until it is ... razor-sharp ... and airtight.

That is, we want to build a solid infrastructure and the beginning of a groundswell before we try to unlock the Big Dude's calendar. Thus, the initial sales emphasis is on folks who can help us take the next, practical step forward ... not the big boss. Another plus: The Suits at the top may well hear a little buzz from below ... and so ... when you finally do approach them with your (field-tested, razor-sharp, airtight) pitch ... the groundswell has been forming, and they'll tend to be more receptive.

(Rule No. 1: Smart project champions keep bosses at bay until the time is ripe! Paradoxically, this is especially true if things are going well: We don't want to be co-opted until we're good and ready.)

T.T.D./Sell to Peers First!

1. Now ... re-do "the elevator spiel" (No. 22 above) into a "corridor pitch" for peers.

2. Practice it. On anybody. Everybody.

3. Tape it. Video record it. Play it back for yourself. What works? What doesn't? Are *you* sold?

4. So ...

go sell.

24.

Do T-shirts for teammates when milestones are hit ("The All-Night Gang" ... etc.) Or buttons for an upcoming presentation ("WOW Team") ... or ... whatever.

The Nub

A marketing pitch (sales pitch) that works is about inevitability, about irresistibility: "This is **the** cool (WOW!) project!" "We are doing some **seriously neat stuff** here!"

And: "Inevitable" and "irresistible" are the products of our hard work. I.e., a conscious effort to "make a stir," to "create buzz" around our ever more WOW-worthy Project.

There are a thousand tools. (Just ask Avon or Tupperware or Amway.) It's the T-shirts. (Team WOW!/Team Cool!/Purchasing Pirates!/etc.) *And* the mugs. *And* the buttons. *And* the caps. *And* the pens. If nothing is going on ∴ the buttons won't help. But if it *is* a Cool Deal, parading your team's spunk is a matchless sales/marketing—not to mention morale-building—ploy.

T.T.D./Planned Pizzazz

1. Focus—consciously—on fun, fury, energy, pizzazz, momentum. What specific (internal or external) "marketing"/"sales"/"buzz" activity have you performed ... *in the last **48** hours?*

2. Keep the T-shirts (buttons, jackets, etc.) coming! At least once a week do something—concrete—that calls attention to/"advertises"/boosts the project ... and its most recent milestone/signed-up customer/new teammate.

3. Start a Friday-at-two-o'clock e-mail (*"The Weekly WOW!"*) that goes to everyone even peripherally involved in your project.

25.

Talk your "it" up everywhere. (WOW Project champions never meet an audience that's too small!) Present the project to a wider audience. *Yield:* Take community concerns into account. *But:* DON'T COMPROMISE THE DREAM. Know when to advance. *And* when to retreat with grace. But ... NEVER ... EVER ... stop Community Building!

The Nub

You're busy. Your "to do" list is a mile long. Five key tasks are behind schedule. One key team member is threatening to quit. I.e.: The Last Damn Thing you have time for is ... lunch with the guy who this other guy recommended to you ... who might be a "good bet to know a [test] site possibility."

S o o o o o o o : *Go to lunch with the guy!*

That is: *Never—ever!—neglect "community building."* WOW Projects feed on a growing web of supporters. You must—always!—be in the "hustling" **(suck up!)** mode. Sure ... your "substantive"/operational duties could absorb the energy of a platoon. No matter. Make-the-damn-time-to-do-community-building. It's called politics ... Building Bridges ... Forging Alliances ... Making Friends ... Neutralizing Enemies. It's called WOW Project success!

Addendum: Long shot, would-be supporters are almost as good as sure things. ***Any "audience"—of one or more—is an unabashed opportunity for you to proselytize.*** To tell your story to someone new. No, this particular connection may not pan out. But … a *friend* of this guy's may hear about your story … and get enthused … and lend a helping hand … or $$$$.

T.T.D./Community Building Mania!

1. Make a Target List of at least **25** potential supporters. Have all team members contribute to the list. Read up on them, talk to friends and acquaintances: Gather (lots of) data on each of the 25. I.e., DO YOUR "COMMUNITY" RESEARCH … M-E-T-I-C-U-L-O-U-S-L-Y! (See Harvey MacKay's "MacKay 66" in *Swim with the Sharks Without Being Eaten Alive.* This questionnaire is a matchless guide as to what you ought to know when you attempt to recruit/sell someone … on anything.)

2. Schedule a lunch—**call now!**—with **one** would-be supporter from the "25List."

Keep calling prospects until you get at least three lunches scheduled in the next two or three weeks!

3. Ask your pals which Cool People you should be chatting up about your project. Ask them if they'll make a call—send e-mail—to introduce you. Create a "Community-to-Be"/"Community-in-Waiting" prospect list.

4. Work the list! **Daily!** Relentlessly!

26.

It matters not if they signed on early ... or late. A supporter is a supporter. Period. It's called pragmatism. It's called results. It's called selling Revolutionary-WOW.

Welcome that Johnny/Janie-Come-Lately with (sincere) open arms. Of course, your nervy early supporters have a special place in your heart. But ... if some old S.O.B. ... who wouldn't give you the time of day ... can be lured on board to contribute to your eventual triumph ... go get him! (P.S.: It's one of Bill Clinton's secrets. Impeach him? Fine. He'll still reach w-a-y out and work with 'em, because his legacy is on the line.)

The Nub

You think ever so fondly about your early supporters. And ever-so-angrily about those who sneered. And jeered.

Fine. It's normal.

But ... now ... there's a little buzz going around the project. And an early rejecter—apparently oblivious to his past—calls and says he'd "love to talk to you about the project. Can you spare a lunch?"

Answer: **You damn well can!** (And will!)

On board is on board. **Period!** Of course, you'll most love those who stuck their necks out for you at the beginning. But as time (and the project) moves on, you'll need a larger, more "normal"/well-rounded community. **Period.** So forgive (if not forget) and embrace the latecomer/former naysayer with the vigor of the father's embrace of the prodigal son.

T.T.D./ **Love** Janie-Come-Lately!

1. Six months into your project and with success stories in your kit, turn the other cheek and take the initiative: Call three or four of the folks who rebuffed you in the early days. Wipe the slate clean. Forgive (tell them that "anybody in their right mind would have been a skeptic six months ago") ... and ask them to lunch ... or for a meeting. Go prepared: Have a specific suggestion as to how they can help/get involved, initially in a minor way. (Hook 'em ... for real. That's the gambit.)

2. Invite one or two of those skeptics to be on your Advisory Board. **The skeptic-turned-visible-advisor (i.e., born again) is a potent signal to others that the mainstream is giving you some attention.** It also elevates you above pettiness and marks you as a person of stature/integrity/character capable of assembling support that spans from top to bottom to sideways.

3. Repeat this exercise every few weeks.

F O R E V E R .

27.

Don't take supporters for granted. Keep them informed. Ask for feedback on anything and everything.

I.e.: KEEP THEM PUMPED! USE THEM!

The Nub

It is sooooo easy to take supporters for granted. Hey, they're supporters. They "get it."

No. No. No. No. No.

Keeping supporters pumped/"in the loop"/engaged is hard, time-consuming work ... *and* worth it. (Understatement.)

Supporters may well "get it," but they need to be **s-h-o-w-e-r-e-d** with attention, kept in the know, and asked for help. Remember: No one has your passion for the project except, perhaps, the core band-of-pirates. Others' interest will atrophy or even, out of pique (from being ignored), turn sour. *So you must ... again* and *again* and *again ... and then* again ... *find ways to re-engage your natural allies. Once more: Think politics. Protect your base!*

1. Concoct a plan!

ALLY-MAINTENANCE IS NOT CATCH-AS-CATCH-CAN WORK! IT IS "STRATEGIC RELATIONSHIP MAINTENANCE."

And it demands a strategic plan … worthy of the value of your supporters … who are, indeed, worth their weight in gold. (Or something far more precious.)

2. Who *are* your allies? Start with great record-keeping. (Perhaps good-but-simple database management software will help. But a great filing card—paper! —system is just dandy … even in … The New Millennium.) Know as much as you can about each ally. Keep adding to the database. *R-e-l-i-g-i-o-u-s-l-y.*

3. Develop "push" programs—e-mail, faxes, mailings—for keeping supporters up-to-date. Consider a regular "In the Loop" e-mail/fax/memo, which briefly summarizes project highlights for the week and plans for next week. Be succinct, interesting (tell stories), and *solicit feedback.* (E-feedback.) (You don't want anyone to think he or she is just one more name on some form mailing.)

4. Plan a stream of Special Events. Some will be big: sneak previews, complete with banners and balloons. Some will be small: informal "roundtable" lunches with four or five key supporters.

5. Create a **"Supporters Management Program."** Assign a team member as "buddy" to each key supporter: *It's her/his (c-l-e-a-r) (and monitored) respon-sibility to keep the key supporter feeling a part of the team.*

6. Work at creating a sense of exclusivity/*really*-in-the-loop. Provide critical supporters with, say, Special Previews or Feedback Sessions not available to others. Give them the sense of being co-designers.

7. Put "Strategic Management of Supporters" on the agenda of the Weekly Operating Review. I.e., integrate strategic supporter management into the "culture"/ "business systems" of the project.

* * *

HINT: **This is one of the key areas where busy project-management teams falter. (They're too busy with the "substance.") Only solution: IT MUST BE MANAGED!**

* * *

IT'S THE SUPPORTERS, STUPID! Dateline, November 2, 1998. *San Jose Mercury News*, Page 1-A: "It made sense to find [California gubernatorial candidate] Gray Davis and U.S. Senator Barbara Boxer in black churches and union halls on Sunday. That's where Democrats go on the Sunday before an election to rally their most loyal voters." (P.S.: They both won big. Again: Stroke your b-a-s-e, they deserve it… and you *need* them. I.e.: You need their vigorous, visible support.)

* * *

It's the supporters, stupid!

28.

Surround 'em! Marginalize 'em! Forget 'em!

The Nub

We've focused on friends. Finding 'em. Loving 'em up. But what about foes? (All worthy change programs— that is, WOW Projects—have them.)

I have always hated the management literature on "overcoming resistance to change." Why? Because I don't think it's the way *real* change agents—e.g., community organizers, leaders in business, politics, the arts—work.

They don't try to "overcome objections." Instead they follow what one pal of mine (a successful organizer from Cleveland, involved in that city's renaissance) calls the "surround and marginalize" strategy.

Those who plan mass revolts ... or union-certification drives ... or are missionaries for a particular religion ... play the game according to one rule: *Start with would-be zealots; continue through lukewarm but susceptible types; forget your enemies until you (your project) becomes "in- evitable" ... and t-h-e-n shower the heathen with kindness and welcome them belatedly into the fold.*

The most effective change-agents ignore the barbs and darts. They build ... and build ... and build. **Then they b-u-i-l-d some more.** Their time is spent on allies and likely allies. (Period.) And if they do it right, the allies become the mainstream and eventually "the enemy" becomes an island.

There is a normal, human tendency to "take on" (or, worse by far, "take on publicly") someone who opposes you. Particularly if that detractor has sounded off in public. But ... it is such a dreadful waste of time, energy, and resources! **The** waste of time, energy, and resources! And, most important, such a waste of our most crucial resource ... emotional capital.

And if that's not enough, attacking enemies may unnecessarily (1) turn off buddies of your "enemy" who are *not* opposed to your project, and (2) get you labeled in general as a "precious little shit who deserves to be kicked."

To be sure, competition is the spice of life. "Winning" is a great motivator. And it's also tragic but true—more for testosterone-laden guys than women—that part of the motivational edge is that "the other guy" loses! While I support the motivation of potential victory over the forces of (corporate, say) reaction, I still contend that fighting enemies is a foolish waste of energy; you're reading the words of a passionate guy [me] whose tongue is permanently bloody from all the times I've bitten it ... after deciding not to pick a fight or rejoin a particularly nasty barb. (But, hey, after "it" is over, go ahead and visit the pub with your early mates ... and dis the Infidels.)

T.T.D./Ignore Thine Enemies!

1. Spend your scarce time garnering more s-u-p-p-o-r-t-e-r-s ... and don't obsess on "scoring points" during that presentation to a clear nonsupporter. It's not going to convince him anyway ... at least not at this point in the project's development.

2. Work with that wise elder/advisor. (See No. 19 above.) Spend time (lots of) with her. She will probably help you (a lot) on this: I.e., will help keep your anger at "enemies" from turning your project into a vendetta ... which will, in the process, quickly destroy your (hard-won, growing, fragile) credibility. **Vendettas are not pretty to watch ... and typically backfire on both parties.** Anger is usually a very destructive emotion ... and a very tricky motivator. WOW works best when it comes from a positive place: Hey, you're creating great things here; screw 'em (a.k.a. forget about them) if they can't see, appreciate, and hop on the WOW-Wagon.

Antagonistic (Ants) Waste Precious Energy!

"The good guys really do come out ahead, at least in the ant world," researchers said last week.

A team at the University of California-San Diego in La Jolla said that they had found that peaceful ants are more prosperous and long-lived than their warring neighbors.

It seems that waging war and guarding territory waste time and resources better used for making babies and finding food, David Holway and colleagues reported in the journal Science.

—The San Jose Mercury News, November 3, 1998

29.

This is a must for big (or biggish) projects ... and a good idea for all but the smallest activities.

The Advisory Board adds credibility and *becomes a sales team unto itself.*

A board of three is fine, but at some stage it could grow to dozens when you're trying to ... Sell the World.

The Nub

This is a subset of the supporters' idea. Remember: We're talking "sales" in this section. And a/the key to sales is credibility/"branding." And: A blue-chip Advisory Board can help ...

a lot!

Consider a mailing you get, from a group you don't know, asking for money. Assuming you don't automatically toss it, one of the first things you're likely to do—I do this religiously—is look at the left side of the letterhead ... where you'll invariably find the Board of Directors/Advisory Board. In most cases, if it's familiar, laced with interesting or stellar personalities in their fields, you'll at least read on.

In short: *We're as good as those we associate with.* Or, more accurately:

We are **perceived** to be as good as those who are willing to **publicly** associate with us!

If all this sounds like advice to those raising funds for a Community Center, it is. (Of course.) But it's also true, with perhaps a little more informality, for those seeking support to revamp a business system inside a division of a company.

If we're up to something truly "cool"—i.e., that vaporizes applecarts—we need the establishment's cover. The good news: Even "the establishment" has a few (at least semi-) freaks (or freak sympathizers) who may be willing to hang their cashmere scarves next to our scruffy baseball caps.

Maybe, in the case of the division's process revision, you don't list your Advisory Board on the letterhead. But do—visibly—gather them upon occasion, keep them in the loop (tightly!), and use their names around others who need to hear that you have ... ***Weighty Supporters*** ... before they'll sign on. Even in the case of an internal process revision, you will benefit, at some point, by formalizing the advisor process. I.e.: Ask your Establishment Supporters if you can formally refer to them as an Advisory Group, or Board of Wise Elders, or Project Angels, or whatever.

In bigger projects, this process can become more elaborate. That is, you might start with a tiny, Very-Blue-Chip board of advisors ... and gradually build to a formal, but B-team, advisory list that numbers in the dozens ... or even a hundred. Again: The advisors are your Trust Mark/Certification/Establishment Seal of Approval.

т.т.d./Blue Chip Advisor Power!

1. Very early on ... start recruiting a small number of Blue Chip/Establishment supporters. If your Rolodex is slim here, ask friends who their friends are. Typical early advisors may not be, say, senior corporate officers ... but, instead, well-known "cool people" who are admired for their pioneering spirit. Get these would-be "advisors" engaged in the project-definition process.

I.e., pander!

2. Formalize—small "f" or Big "F"—the Advisory Board/Advisory Group/Project Angels process. Ask three or four of your Credible Converts if they will informally (or formally) "serve" as an Advisory Board/Reference Group. Also at this juncture, formalize the use of and communication with the Advisory Group: Make sure its members receive, say, regular briefings (e-mail, etc.) and/or are invited to bimonthly or quarterly face-to-face meetings.

3. At first, the board will be Fellow Zealots who love you and your cause. In due time, expand the board to include carefully chosen representatives of key constituencies—e.g., the finance department—who will be engaged in large-scale project execution and roll out. (*Reminder:* Consistent with earlier advice, when you do reach out to, say, Finance, look for a sympathetic Young Turk who will actively work with you ... not necessarily a formally "powerful" person.)

4. Once you have established the Advisory Board, you must spend time on the nurturance thereof.

THIS IS TIME YOU **CAN (MUST!)** SPEND ... NO MATTER HOW "BUSY" YOU ARE WITH THE "SUBSTANCE."

(Hint: This *is* substance!—that is, gaining credible support *and* the appearance thereof.)

5. Hide nothing from your Advisory Board! These Credibility Keepers can be the most help when you have setbacks. (Which you will ... regularly.) But the Advisors will be less likely to rush to your aid ... if you've hidden the problems—technical, financial, personnel—from them. (And that's an understatement!)

30.

In startups, one tries hard not to sell 50 percent of the company ... early on ... for peanuts. So, too, in WOW Project land. You don't want to sell your soul/independence too soon. The alternative? *Learn to live off the land!* I.e.: *SCROUNGE!* Borrow a few PCs here, a workspace there, for a month or two (or ten!). Do your Quick Prototyping (see below) on-the-cheap.

The Nub

No baloney: **MONEY** (too early, too much) **KILLS INITIATIVE + INDEPENDENCE.**

There's a lot to recommend the scrounger/bootstrapper mentality. E.g.:

* You must rush to get demonstrable results (no resources to waste!).

* You can choose your own allies, especially freaks and renegades (you are—mostly—beholden to no one).

* You can invent the project your way.

* You can dream big **(B-I-G)**.

* When you're 25 percent done, you can toss it all out and start again if you need to. (This is nigh onto impossible if you're beholden to someone.)

My most successful "corporate" project, at McKinsey & Co., benefited from being: (1) *poorly* funded, (2) *far away* from the New York headquarters, (3) blessed by *low expectations* about payoff. It truly freed/empowered us to: (1) shoot for the moon and (2) recruit cool-but-largely-powerless supporters.

I'm also convinced that the "scrounger" mentality sharpens one's creative powers immensely. There's no possibility of gold plating … so one cuts to the (simple/basic) heart of the matter. Plus, money breeds lassitude, long lunches, a less-is-on-the-line mentality—all premier WOW-Killers.

It's a bit of a paradox: Low funding means (1) you've got to produce quickly with limited resources *and* (2) you're free to d-r-e-a-m in an unrestricted fashion precisely because you are not (**!**) beholden to anyone.

It is very simple: In my experience, the throw-money-at-it projects are always under the establishment's electron microscope … and almost always produce incremental, non-risky results. While the underfunded project doesn't always result in a home run … virtually all home runs begin as underfunded projects. Go figure!

T.T.D./Scrounge, Baby, Scrounge!

1. You think I'm nuts. But … **truly** … listen to the masters I've listened to: Watch out for the strings attached to lots of early bucks. (Those strings *are* there ... no matter what the donor says!)

2. Cobble together the resources (people, space, tools) by recruiting Passionate Sponsors ... **o f t e n u n - p o w e r f u l** ... *who are in-desperate-love with your "it." (Love/commitment/passion beats cash ... early on ... and usually later on, too.)*

3. Avoid any and all signs of ostentation. There's nothing uglier than "revolutionaries" living high off the hog; you want to give off the vibes of the Determined Worldbeaters ... in sackcloth.

4. Instill a "culture of scrounging" among your team-mates. Look for cool volunteers. Look for cheap work-spaces. Put together Quick Prototypes from sows' ears (see below, and also our forthcoming *the Quick Proto-type50*).

5. Try these "Scroungers Laws":

* Revolutionaries fly coach!

* Live lite! Dream grand!

* Question authority! Don't sell out! We don't want your tainted money! *(Yet.)*

* Recruit "cool." Ignore "powerful."

* Scrounge, baby, scrounge!

* Quick Prototype your way to glory!

* Anything that "takes a month" can be done in two days!

WOW Projects and the pursuit of venture capital have everything in common. I've just sung the praises of modest initial WOW Project funding (e.g., funding that allows you to seek WOW with no strings attached). The same is true when a business is searching for startup capital; it doesn't want to be flooded with money that it will be tempted to blow on fancy offices and other perks. It wants to stay hungry and (to the highest possible degree) unbeholden.

But the funding/venturing parallel goes much further. WOW Project funding overall perfectly mirrors the stages of venture funding. E.g.:

1. Start with seed money, scrounged from this pot or that.

2. Seek customer (pioneer/"lead" user) input and resources for an early prototype or two.

3. Seek Round No. 1 "venture support" (from your boss ... or somebody else's boss) which permits you to use the prototype results, say, as the basis for rolling out the project in one out of 11 "districts."

4. Finally, seek CEO/Division Chief support for corporate rollout ... once that regional effort has proven itself.

Message: **Keep your freedom/flexibility!** (Virtually at all costs.) Aim for successive rounds of practical results. "Sell out" in stages ... with increasing successes to justify your Controlling Role in the next stage.

31.

One more time:

You are not looking for "best" customers; you are looking for customers who love you … a.k.a. are excited-as-all-get-out about the project.

In fact, paradoxically, it's best if these first customers are *not* high profile … and (maybe) live a long way from home. (*Axiom:* It's always best to test new/weird stuff in the boonies!)

The Nub

Sales success = Great "demos." Great "demos" = Results from *real* customer tests subject to *real* conditions.

"Sales" rules! So: You need a "track record." **ASAP**. So: You need "real" tests. So: You need *real*/freaky-cool customers … **ASAP** … who will test (and testify to) your prototypes. And then … soon … you will need a few more *real*/not-*quite*-so-freaky customers who will test (and testify to) your not-*quite*-so-early prototypes.

Bottom line: "Sales"—e.g., lassoing more and more committed supporters—depends upon results of more and more realistic tests/approximations of your WOW Project's "deliverables."

(Big-league version of this: Microsoft had 300,000 "Beta Site" testers for Windows95 ... who provided, according to one estimate, about one-*billion* dollars worth of free advice—time!—to the software Goliath.)

T.T.D./First "Real" Customers!

1. On day No. 1—or no later than day No. 2—shuffle through your Rolodex looking for a tiny handful of potential "first users." Put together a rough—but WOW!—briefing and meet with them. Try to sign up one (or two) to be a first-partial-test site(s). Maybe you can even get them so enthused they'll lend you one of their folks for a few days/weeks to work with you!

2. Turn this exercise into something more systematic: In your wanderings, seek out a few more potential users ... and then a few more:

Quickly build a Pioneer Users Group.

Message: Forming a users association need not—should not!—wait until full-scale roll-out! Exploit your Pioneer Users Group for project development and supporter-sign-up and buzz-creation purposes.

REPRISE: SELL!

IRON LAW:

Effective Dreamers/WOW Project Champions are full-time Salespersons.

Period.

This is the wrap-up of PART II … so I'm going back to square one … my first point … the BIG ONE … so please …

LISTEN UP!

My No. 1 gripe with the project-management types (okay, No. 2, after the absence of "WOW") (Okay, tied for second, along with not talking about the "create" dimension): the failure to acknowledge that "project management" **is** sales.

Selling. *Not a dirty word.* It means gaining support … and support*ers* … in ever-increasing numbers. Ad infinitum.

So you're not a "sales guy" (gal). B-a-l-o-n-e-y. We're *all* "sales guys" … if—**if!**—we care enough about our project. (E.g., community center.) (E.g., form redesign … yes, there *is* passion in the form redesign. Remember: thin end of the b-i-g wedge to change "the way we do things around here.") If you love your project … and you *must* love your project if there's even a smidgen of hope for WOW … then the importance of s-e-l-l-i-n-g (it) should be imperative/obvious.

What I'm trying to "sell" here is a "sales mentality."

Winners
—WOW Project winners—
are, even if reluctantly,
Sales Maniacs.

Which means they can't resist the urge to Spread the Word about their pet project. Moreover—even if reluctantly—they don't shy away from the word "sales."

I.e.: **S - e - l - l !**

III. implement!

III. **Implementation means a detailed plan. Right?** *Right!* **Clear assignments of responsibility?** *Right again!* **But ... again ... that's little more than the least of it.**

Things (conditions, resources, people) change all the time. Especially these (insanely, absurdly, comically) volatile days.

So implementation means ... staying flexible ... and adjusting your plan as necessary. It means ... mastering the Art of Quick Prototyping.

Effective implementers (project managers) move forward by test-test-test-*adjust*-test-test-test-*adjust* ... ad infinitum ... ad nauseum ... until they get it more or less *right!* ... for now.

They eschew—laugh at—the bankrupt B-School notion of religiously following the plan-plan-plan-plan-'til-you're-blue-in-the-face route. (And, um, then plan some more.)

Thus, selling (the topic of the previous section) and implementing are integrated from Day One of the WOW Project. They have a symbiotic relationship: Implementation responds to the results of selling/prototyping/cool-customer-feedback; and the ever-more-encompassing-sales pitch is continuously fine-tuned in response to adjustments made as implementation and prototyping move into high gear.

Implementation's primary goal is actually ... **more sales.** Roping in more and more ... and ever more ... enthusiastic supporters as we go along.

But that's not all ...

32.

We've gotta break "it"—our project, now on the move—down into tidbit/do-it-today/do-it-in-the-next-four-hours pieces.

The good news: You *can* do it if you put your mind to it! The mindset of "action now" will make or break the one-day or five-year project.

The Nub

"Chunk it." My pal and colleague Bob Waterman (co-author of *In Search of Excellence*) said this first. And hit the nail square on the head.

Chunking. Chunks. To chunk. Chunk-mania. To break it up. To find a ... small ... very small ... itty-bitty piece of the puzzle you can play with, test, and learn something from ... now ... immediately ... instantly. The fantastic added benefit from chunking is the sense of *momentum* and *accomplishment* it creates. Every day *something* ... concrete ... gets *tested* (not just talked about or planned); and project energy and drive increase exponentially. And if the chunk-test fails, hey, it failed quickly—so move on! (Is there anything more enervating to WOW! than a long, circuitous talkfest where a lot of high-sounding theory is thrown around ... and when the gabfest is over, you're not an inch closer to fruition/"doin' real stuff"?)

It is so—damn!—obvious. But if it *is* so obvious … then why are so few people/organizations good at it? Why do the great majority spend months on elaborate plans before trying something—some wee thing—in the real world?

Successful WOW-ing (as in WOW Projects, creation thereof) is about wholes. Successful *implementation* is about *de*-construction. Crack a little bit off the project. Any bit. Tiny bit. **Now.** Test it. Somewhere. Somehow. **Now.** Learn something. Adjust. **Now.** And then … break off a new … little … chunk. And test it. And …

Progress via chunk-and-test is, in short, **the essence** of effective project execution.

T.T.D./Chunk Mania!

1. Now. **Right now.** Take some little—tiny! —element of your project. Corral a surrogate customer. Talk to him/her about it. That is … test it. Now. (That is: Welcome to … Chunk Channel.)

2. Your immediate goal: "Chunk up" the next three weeks. I.e.: Define a set of practical micro-bits … that can be subjected to real-world tests …

A.S.A.P.I.N.S.

(**A**s **S**oon **A**s **P**ossible **I**f **N**ot **S**ooner.)

33.

Observation:

There is *no* situation—even at Boeing—where you cannot concoct a sorta-real-world micro-test of some piece of your project…**within a few hours to two or three days. Quick Prototyping Excellence = Project Implementation Excellence.** (No kidding…it's almost that basic!)

The Nub

The idea of No. 32: a generic instinct to crack project implementation into v-e-r-y small bits. Chunks. And No. 33 is **the** tool for testing those chunks: the

Quick Prototype.

We think it's so central to WOW Projects that it will be the subject of another (full) book in this series: *the Quick Prototype50.*

TOP PRIORITY?????????????

Say "project"/"project management" and … what comes to mind?

Well…here are the first five questions from the "Project Management Excellence Questionnaire" (excerpted from *In Search of Excellence in Project Management*):

"1. My company *actively* uses the following processes:

   A. Total Quality Management (TQM) only.

   B. Concurrent engineering (shortening deliverable development time) only.

   C. TQM and concurrent engineering only.

   D. Risk management only.

   E. Risk management and concurrent engineering only.

   F. Risk management, concurrent engineering, and TQM.

"2. On what percent of your projects do you use the principles of total quality management?

   A. Zero percent.

   B. 5—10 percent.

   C. 11—25 percent.

   D. 26—50 percent.

   E. 51—75 percent.

   F. 76—100 percent.

"3. On what percent of your projects do you use the principles of risk management?

   A. Zero percent…

   F. 76—100 percent.

"**4.** On what percent of your projects do you try to compress product/deliverable schedules by performing work in parallel rather than in series?

    A. Zero percent…

    F. 76—100 percent.

"**5.** My company's risk management process is based upon:

    A. We do not use risk management.

    B. Financial risks only.

    C. Technical risks only.

    D. Scheduling risks only.

    E. A combination of financial, technical, and scheduling risks based upon the project…."

It's not that these are silly questions. (They aren't.) It's just that they miss the point. *The whole point.* Surprise (that is, no surprise): WOW, Beauty, Reframing, Sales, and Buzz are missing. And so … of course is Quick Prototyping.

"The book"—*In Search of Excellence in Project Management*—makes it all seem so dreary. Project management…dreary? That's what "the books" say. And me? I think it's so…

thrilling … challenging … exhilarating … goosebumpy, short-hair-tingly, blood-racingly … cool.

And coolness—in project implementation—is at heart... Quick Prototyping Mania.

SERIOUS PLAY

The perfect antidote to *In Search of Excellence in Project Management* is innovation guru—my innovation guru!—Michael Schrage's brilliant, new, original, undreary **Serious Play.** *Topic:* Prototyping! *Theme:* A "culture" of rapid prototyping is the ultimate marker of *any* innovative organization. (As I said in my foreword to that book ... I believe it is the best book on innovation I've ever read.)

* * *

Image: finger painting in a kindergarten classroom. *Image:* a National Football League Tuesday-walk-through-practice session. *Image:* an investment bank's acquisition team creating reams of spreadsheets with dozens... and dozens ... of possible deal structures. *Image:* a theater company holding a staged reading of a new play. *Image:* the local barbershop quartet sitting in The Old Station restaurant in Pawlet, Vermont, singing a song they're considering adding to their repertoire.

It's all the same: **trying stuff** ... quick approximations ... rough-and-ready run-throughs. It's progress-via-trial-error-adjustment-trial. Always: **a-c-t-i-o-n**.

"Practice" is the essence of the arts (sports, theater, etc.) and ... oddly ... almost entirely absent in business.

(And certainly absent in business "literature.") In the arts we imagine something … then try it … then adjust it … then try it again … **ASAP.** In business, and "credit" the business schools to a large extent: We talk … and talk … *and talk some more* … and plan and plan … *and plan some more* … before we head to the practice field. At which point, likely as not, all the WOW has been talked out of our inspiration … and we're left with the "safe" (a.k.a. couldn't-possibly-offend-the-boss-or-any-other-living-human-being) choice.

But the smart ones—like David Kelley of IDEO Design & Product Development and those often maligned I-bankers—live and breathe: play … prototype … trial … adjust … **N-O-W.**

* * *

TECHNICOLOR LIFE = TRIAL A-N-D ERROR
TECHNICOLOR LIFE = QUICK PROTOTYPING

T.T.D./Quick Prototyping Mania!

1. Build a prototype … of some (small) part of your project **. . . in the next three h-o-u-r-s.** (*No joke! We do this in our WOW Project Seminars.*) Test it. Today.

2. Tomorrow. See No. 1 above. I.e.: Repeat! Prototype! Test!

3. Review our *the Quick Prototype50*. Please. (Okay … you'll have to wait a few months. It's scheduled for the next set of *50List* releases.) (In the meantime, click on

Amazon.com and order—overnight delivery!—Michael Schrage's *Serious Play* ... see above.)

Quick Prototyper's Laws

1. Define a small, practical test of some piece of the project ... in a page or less of text. Now.

2. Gather materials already at hand to conduct the test ... on the (very) cheap. Now.

3. Find a (kinky?) partner-customer who will provide a test site and will act as a sounding board. Now.

4. Set a very tight deadline of five working days—or a little more or a little less—for this next, practical step.

5. Conduct the test. ASAP.

6. De-brief and meticulously record the results in the Project Notebook.

7. Set the next test date. ASAP. (In five days.)

8. Repeat ... ad infinitum.

* * *

BIG IDEA: **Establish the *Rhythm* of *Quick Prototyping*.**

QUICK PROTOTYPING: **"It's 'the way we work' around here. It is what we *do*."**

33a.

The Nub

Again: Thanks, Michael Schrage. I'm pretty confident that he invented the term **Culture of Prototyping.** The idea: Prototyping that makes a difference is a **way of life**, not just a procedure.

How did many of us manage to put "quality" into our "corporate cultures"? We studied it. We trained-the-Hell-out-of-it. We jawboned and bully-pulpited it. We rewarded it. I.e., we did everything we could think of to insinuate it into "the way we do business around here." My point: Prototyping (Quick Prototyping) is just as important as quality.

So ... let's go at it hammer and tongs:

* Study!

* Train!

* Practice!

* Practice!

* Practice!

* Reward!

T.T.D./Create a Quick Prototyping Culture

1. Train! Launch serious, full-scale training courses in Quick Prototyping.

2. Benchmark! Study top Quick Prototypers such as Sony and IDEO and HP and 3M and Yahoo.

3. Talk! Talk up Quick Prototyping … daily.

4. Reward! Put Quick Prototyping Mastery into the formal evaluation process … for everyone.

34.

The Chunk + Quick Prototype Mindset is mirrored in a culture that cherishes playfulness. (Yes ... in the Purchasing Department!)

Play is serious stuff! Just watch a four-year-old "at work" ... uh, play. I call it "the spirit of the sandbox."

Hint: Playfulness is the essence of the sober, scientific method, where there is only one true mantra: *Try It! Now! I.e.: P-l-a-y with it!*

Corollary: Find playmates. **Spirited play calls for spirited playmates ... a.k.a. those first precious customers, who will road test your 1/64th-baked prototypes.** (Such "customers" can include pals you corral in the hallway ... and who agree to give you 45 minutes to "walk through a little mockup of a process" you just—this morning—created. Bless them!)

The Nub

My No. 1 bugbear: words we use routinely between 5:00 and 9:00 (p.m. to a.m.) ... that we don't dare utter between 9:00 and 5:00 (a.m. to p.m.).

E.g.: **p - l - a - y !**

WOW Project Implementation = Inspired Playfulness. Playfulness is an awesome trait. It's about trusting yourself enough to let go … relax … let the enormous wealth of creativity that lives inside every single one of us break out. You'll discover an enormous Personal Competitive Advantage. (It makes me chortle … *so much* … to dream about the word "Play" showing up in the index to a traditional project management book. Not in this lifetime!)

Play is not "funny." Play is serious. Proof? Watch that four-year-old at work on a sand castle. Watch the intensity … the absorption … the determination … the complete and total lack of self-consciousness. Test. Destroy. Test again. *Destroy again.* Modify. Engagement? Sky-high! (Fail to keep your eye on the kid … and he/she could be washed out to sea with the next tide. Literally.) Goal-obsessed? You'd best believe it!

So … *enjoy yourself!*

Go for it! Try it! Blow it up! Try it again! Ah … progress. Ah … p-l-a-y.

PROPONENTS OF PLAY

DEEP PLAY: (dēp), adj. (plā), n. 1. A state of unselfconscious engagement with our surroundings. 2. An exalted zone of transcendence over time. 3. A state of optimal creative capacity.

—Diane Ackerman, *Deep Play*

You can't be a serious innovator unless and until you are ready, willing, and able to seriously play. "Serious play" is not an oxymoron; it is the essence of innovation.
—Michael Schrage, *Serious Play*

T.T.D./The Playground Rules!

1. Talk with your teammates about play. If our project were a playground ... what would we do differently? Right now? **(Ten ideas, please!)** Take some dull/dull-ish detail of your project. *Play* with it. Reconceive it. Do something with it that's wild, woolly, unexpected. Try it. See how it, uh, plays.

2. Talk with your key users (your playmates!) about ... p·l·a·y. How can we turn our next test into something that's playful, so that user-playmates can let their imaginations soar and supply you with playful (a.k.a. inspired, unexpected, quirky, worth-its-weight-in-gold) feedback?

3. All together: Evaluate our WOW Project Team ... on Play Skill. (E.g.: Are we being genuinely playful in pursuing our dream?)

35.

All this—chunk-it/prototype mania/play fanaticism—is about Fast Feedback and dramatically shortening feedback loops. *WOW Projects live off almost instant test-and-feedback-and-adjustment cycles!*

Reward success and failure equally. Punish inactivity.
—David Kelley, IDEO Design & Product Development

Ready. Fire! Aim. —Ross Perot (and others such as Harry Quadracci, founder, Quad/Graphics, and Wayne Calloway, former PepsiCo chairman)

The Nub

Can you tell: **I'M TRYING MY DAMNEDEST TO RAM "R.F.A." (Ready. Fire! Aim.) AND "QP" (Quick Prototyping) DOWN YOUR THROAT (and into your brain) ... TO MAKE IT CLEAR ... THAT THIS—not "the plan"—IS IMPLEMENTATION ISSUE/ TOOL/OPPORTUNITY NO. 1.**

"Fail. Forward. Fast":

A high-tech exec calls that his mantra. The goal: Compress the execution timeframe and feedback loops exponentially! (Exponentially: right word. Michael Schrage's meticulous studies demonstrate that the rabid prototypers are *hundreds* of times faster than the slugabed/specification-obsessed types.)

To achieve breathtaking speed you've got to squeeze the hot air and the horseshit out of the process. (All processes!) That means chilling out on the talk and the ego. Got an idea? Get off your butt and test/prototype it ...**N-O-W!**

And don't worry about who gets credit. (You can fight over that later—and WOW Projects produce enough credit and glory to go around.) Get it out there and get some responses ... **N-O-W!** Digest those responses and make adjustments based on them ... **N-O-W!** At every turn, at every corner, at every opportunity, cut the crap, can the chat, eschew the credit:

JUST STICK WITH THE CONCRETE, GET THE DAMN JOB DONE, AND KEEP THE PROJECT M-O-V-I-N-G!

This is particularly true for the WOW Project. That is: WOW is a subjective judgment. It's about art/beauty ... and things that take your (and your customers') breath away. You can only have your breath taken away if there is something r-e-a-l to react to. (*Right? Think about it.*)

WOW is about 100 false starts ... until we get the thing j-u-s-t r-i-g-h-t e-x-c-r-u-c-i-a-t-i-n-g-l-y c-o-o-l. A hundred false starts demand a ferocious, fast test-and-adjust-and-retest-mentality. Or death do us part!

T.T.D./Fail. Forward. Fast.

1. *Manage* your test-and-adjust cycle. Beware too much Monday-morning quarterbacking. Quickly evaluate your last test. (No blame. Just the facts.) Incorporate a (very) few key changes. *And:* Get-it-out-there-again-in-the-real-world.

2. Post-test:

Write up the feedback ... **within 24 hours.**

Incorporate changes ... **within 24 hours.**

Go again ... **within 24 hours.**

This is the metric/syncopated/momentum-making pace you are trying to establish. And maintain. (*And:* It can be done.)

36.

Ask an artist: Only a willingness to destroy an almost-finished piece of work will lead to WOW!

The Nub

You're two-fifths of the way through the project. It doesn't sing. You test ... and try some more. "Okay." But no "gasp" of greatness. So: *Blow it up.* Scrap it. At the very least ... set it aside.

Blow it up = Go-back-to-square-one-and-reinvent. It's the essence—often as not—of (eventual) WOW Project success. This can—and will—be hard. We all grow attached to some part of our projects; after all, that's Our Baby you're talking about.

The challenge: Let go of that old demon ego and junk the whole damn thing. (It ain't WOW ... and you know it.) There's a moment of (wretched) agony and then (usually) a terrific sense of ... relief ... elation ... and a surge of energy that pushes you to try anew.

A friend who is a successful novelist and professor admonishes her writing students: **"Kill your darlings."** What she means is that if a section of a novel doesn't work, you have to cut it ... no matter how much you love individual sentences and passages. Good advice.(No: Great advice!) A beautiful *piece* of a project is useless—worse than useless, it's destructive—unless it supports the whole. It's the whole that delivers the WOW. I.e.: Destroy and conquer!

And if you *don't* have the nerve? Well … sorry to say … you're simply not in the WOW Project business.

THROW IT AWAY, SAM!

"The real artist," a professional musician friend said, "is willing to risk it all—three months' work—on the next brush stroke."

TOM COMMENT: So, too, the WOW-obsessed.

T.T.D./ Blow It Up!

1. Halt from time to time—monthly?—and ask yourself if you are … no delusions … doing WOW. And—much tougher—ask yourself if you ought to continue with the project. Ask this question seriously … **very** seriously. And if the answer is "no," kill the project swiftly and surely.(Please consider it. This project is *the* signature of your life … eh?)

2. How about a week devoted to some mostly mindless chore you've neglected? A week, that is, away from t-h-e p-r-o-j-e-c-t … so you can approach "it" with a fresh eye … mind … and spirit.(This is a must for me in all writing projects.)

37.

Full-time help. Part-time assistance. *Corner-a-freak-for-lunch … and then* beg *her/him to give you a hand with a little chore!* Hey … could lead to something big down the road.

The Nub

THE SALES JOB—A.K.A. THE WOW PROJECT'S NET-WORK EXPANSION—NEVER EVER STOPS! TO THE CONTRARY: IT ONLY INTENSIFIES OVER TIME.

Sure, I separate the "sales" phase and "implementation" phase in this model-book. The separation, I must admit, is largely phony! If WOW-is-the-goal, sales-is-life … forever. For that reason you need … *desperately* … folks who are walking-, talking-, bursting-with-energy-and-bravado advertisements for your projects. That is, brashly recruit enthusiasm. Projects that aim to tackle the Regnant Corporate Culture need True Believers. (*Anatole France: "I prefer the errors of enthusiasm to the indifference of wisdom."*)

One (the No. 1?) reason we're doing all the rapid prototyping is to demonstrate—quickly—to would-be supporters that we're doing Seriously Cool Stuff:

"Sign up now . . . or get left out."

That's the subliminal message.

T.T.D./Recruit! Forever!

1. *Never "lose a lunch."* Sure you're busy-up-to-
your-eyeballs. But never—ever!—forget your "sales
goals." "Show your stuff" whenever you can! **Demo
everywhere!** Put on spur-of-the-moment presentations to all groups of one or more would-be supporters!

2. Pay special attention to the so-called powerless.

Message:

**Nobody who loves your stuff is power-
less! They are fans! Bless them! Recruit
them! Use them! (Exploit them!)** More
often than not, raw enthusiasm beats formal "position
power." Give me a true-believer, first-line supervisor over
a lukewarm-supporter VP any day! In the mid- to long-
term I will win to the degree that I can create/use
enthusiasts.

3. Take recruiting v-e-r-y seriously. Make it formal.
Develop a hit/target-list. Go after it. Again: Implementation success = Success at bringing others on board ...
especially enthusiastic others. This calls for a **b-i-g**
(in time spent) investment.

37a.

During the often-daunting, often-dragged-out implementation phase, humor can make the world go
'round—or at least help keep it from falling out of orbit.

The Nub

Humor is the secret weapon of WOW! Nothing ... absolutely *nothing* ... cuts tension and creates unity and a
WOW Culture like humor.

A deadline is barreling toward you at 90 m.p.h. Your
team has consumed enough caffeine to hip-hop all night
long; the place is a stress-fest, a tension-convention.

Suddenly, someone tells a joke or makes a really funny
comment about what you're doing ... or about the donut
he just ate ... or about the Absurdity of Life.

A laugh soars ... yes, **SOARS** ... around the team
room. And it's followed by an emotional ... *renewal* ... and
refreshment ... you can actually feel.

One of the great recent examples of the power of
humor was the speech former senator Dale Bumpers
made in defense of President Clinton during his impeachment trial. It was a masterful speech in many ways;

but it was Bumpers's self-deprecating humor in the midst of all that … gravity and "history" and self-righteous solemnity … that suddenly brought the proceedings down to a human level.

A sample (I paraphrase poorly): "One day in church, the pastor asked if anyone present had ever met a human being as perfect, as selfless, as free of vengefulness, as Jesus Christ. A fellow in the back raised his hand and said: 'My wife's first husband.'" Laughter erupted in the Senate chamber, and the tension dissipated in a very healthy way.

I would hardly classify the impeachment trial as a WOW Project (closer to Theater of the Absurd), but Senator Bumpers certainly showed us the power of humor—and its penetrating roots—to influence the course of events (many called his speech a watershed in the president's favor).

So look—purposefully—to liven up the team. Run across an especially zany/zestful/funny colleague? Ask her/him—on the spot—to get involved with your project … in some-little-way.

Moreover, serious (Change-the-World) project work means getting beaten and battered from time to time. (Not that *un*-often … in truth.) So you need to look for resilience … humor … the ability to laugh off brutal thrashings … in would-be recruits. A sense of humor that's highly developed usually got that way in response to adversity. True. *And* important. Trade a little in the way of "proven necessary skills" for unbridled enthusiasm and sense of humor. Any day!

T.T.D./Purposeful Exuberance!

1. Chat up *one* would-be, offbeat enthusiast. *Today.* Find her/him in your Rolodex ... or by calling pals and asking about their pals who "might be called a little off, a little nutty, a lot funny."

2. Take a chance!

S i g n   u p   a   r e a l   k o o k .

Record as a troublemaker—a zealot—a clown? So what? Or, rather: Just what you need!

(I.E.: SEEK OUT "MISFITS." MISFIT = PRIOR BOSS WAS UPSET THAT HE/SHE UPSET AN APPLECART OR TWO. HOORAY! JUST WHAT WE'VE BEEN LOOKING FOR!)

3. Make "good sense of humor" a major criterion in all your recruiting forays. (E.g.: Former Texas governor Ann Richards puts "sense of humor" at the top of her recruiting criteria list.)

38.

The binder starts just about empty, but with lots of chapter headings/dividers.

Each heading/subject is a major project topic/"deliverable." (You can also have the content on the computer ... and share it via good Groupware ... but the print version is imperative. Don't believe otherwise!)

The Nub

Is there a "get-organized!" side to all this? You bet!

It's just that "getting organized" doesn't mean getting bureaucratic.

Or installing the latest project-management-software. (Which is another way of saying ... getting bureaucratic.) Getting Organized = Tool No. 1 = THE PROJECT BIBLE/NOTEBOOK/BINDER.

It's the oldest—and simplest—tool around. The notebook. **(T-H-E N-O-T-E-B-O-O-K.)** It may end up being three or four fat ring binders. It's the pack rat's dream: It's got e-v-e-r-y-d-a-m-n-t-h-i-n-g in it.

Every little scrap/napkin/torn-out article. It is more diary than planner. It includes the frivolous and foolhardy … and the serious and sober.

Electronic versions are dandy—and may well work for you. But for many of us, it is the three-ring binder that reigns supreme.

T.T.D./ Binder Power!

1. Start. Today. Go out and buy the binders. Pick ones that you like the "feel" of—color, heft, design. Put *e-v-e-r-y-t-h-i-n-g* in it. I.e.: Encourage garbage collecting; who knows when the little newspaper clipping may help at a critical moment?

2. Work on the binder's organization. **The "chapter heads" are important. They are—in effect— the metaphor or organizing scheme for the whole project.**

3. Now: Use *The Binder.*

(1) Encourage everyone to include everything.

(2) Have occasional meetings just to talk over "Binder stuff." That is, to review the oddball observations team members are collecting along the way.

(3) Make this **fun** … as well as important. It's a biggish part of the game called creative-fresh.

39.

The Nub

Lists 101. Recording Secretary 101. Call it the Power of Note Taking. The power of summarizing. Call it ... **p-o-w-e-r.**

In short: No words can adequately describe the power unintentionally acceded to the ...

Brilliant Summarizer!

And to the person who "reluctantly" accepts the job of Note Taker/To-Do List Maker/Agenda Drafter. The "mere" agenda drafter, in fact, largely *sets* the damn agenda ... which is, after all, the skeleton of the Project Plan itself.

This is a power tool.(For the so-called power-*less*.) And it is a key project execution tool:

IN SHORT ... YOU CAN NEVER HAVE TOO MANY LISTS ... OR SUMMARY DOCS. Lists are a summation ... a dramatic

distillation ... of ... well ... *everything:*
What's important to that WOW Project
... where you're heading ... and what
to *do* next!

(No exaggeration: I think a lot of my implementation success, particularly as a raw youth, was a result of Compulsive Summarizing. I.e.: Religiously, no matter how exhausted I might have been after a six-hour marathon meeting, grasping the nettle ... and writing/circulating a **Summary** ... within hours of the meeting's end. It amounts to seizing the initiative automatically and injecting yourself firmly into the center of the debate. And, to be crude about it: It gives you an excuse to be communicating directly with those several levels up the org chart. See more on this big idea in our forthcoming *the Power+Implementation50.*)

T.T.D./Lists ... Lists ... **More Lists!**

1. Make sure there is *always* **(1)** a notetaker's *instant* summary of every meeting; **(2)** a To-Do list. Live ... die ... by ... BRIEF LISTS. (Sure, some lists conflict with other lists. But at least ... if there are lists, you've got succinct, concrete issues and priorities to debate and clarify.)

2. Pet peeve: Don't use sexy software to make lists. The "product" is often gibberish. A Simple List is ... a Simple List. (E.g., use Word, not Excel.)

3. Edit lists ... all the time. Turn lists into "living lists." **WHAT A TOOL!** Get team members to ... religiously ... add their two-cents' worth by co-editing lists. Develop a protocol: Five different people use five different fonts to enter their list edits … whatever/whenever.

4. Special note for the "powerless":

You Ain't!

And this—List & Summary Making—is a "no-brainer" place to very quietly seize the initiative.

* * *

NOTE: I LOVE LISTS & SUMMARIES. AND I WANT YOU TO L-O-V-E/LEARN TO LOVE LISTS & SUMMARIES! I BELIEVE IN ORGANIZATION. I DO NOT BELIEVE THAT MEANS COMPLICATION. LISTS SIMPLIFY, CLARIFY, EDIFY.

POWER FREAKS

GIVE GOOD L-I-S-T.

40.

I call it the "living-to-do list." It *is* humble. But no tool is more important. **N-O-N-E.** Call it Timeline/To-Do List/ Milestone Map.

It must be simple to a fault. (Go ahead, if you wish, and use complex project planning software; but it is this— the "master to-do list"—by which I swear.) (*In blood, if necessary.*)

Anoint yourself: M.M.—Milestone Maniac. Or T.T.—Timeline Tyrant.

The Nub

I recall how I learned the power of timelines. I was working on a startup. We talked ... and talked ... and talked some more. (V-e-r-y useful.) We planned ... and planned ... and planned some more. (V-e-r-y useful.) And then ... one weekend ... I volunteered to draft a "simple" timeline.

WOW! Reality struck!

That is, assigning real (albeit estimated) dates to "stuff that needed doing before other stuff could be done" was a real eye-opener. I learned more—literally!—in a day of intense "timelining" than in a month of abstract planning/discussion. Suddenly everything began to fall into place. I knew exactly *what* needed to be done and *when*. The effect was no less than galvanizing.

It took me over the top. (I was already pretty close to the top.) The timeline ... is ... *it!*

To create a string of dates that need to be knitted together in order to get you to, say, public product launch seven months from now causes you to assess the real probabilities of getting critical tasks done in a specified period of time. "Launch on 11/10/99" sounds innocent as Hell on 11/10/98. But when you lay out the 24 things (or 244 things!) that stand between here and there ... and you discover that, say, one devilishly difficult task has to get done in the ... *next two weeks* (fat chance!) ... well, get ready for an adrenaline kick of epic proportions.

Since "my epiphany" I've become a Timeline Fanatic ... a Timeline Dervish. I think there is no tool more powerful! (*Period!*) **Timelines + Key milestones = No-baloney "planning."** Forget (or relegate) the sexier stuff. I submit that the timeline knows no peers.

(Again: There are complex forms of this. E.g., PERT/Program Evaluation and Review Technique. I got a master's degree in Civil Engineering on the topic. But, also again, the big idea is ... Keep It Simple—and Clear—Stupid. I.e.: Timelines beat PERT charts. Trust me.)

T.T.D./Timeline Tyrant!

1. Knowing *whatever* you know *now* (a little, a lot) draft a timeline extending up to **18 months** out. Sure, many/most/all of the latter dates are WAGs (wild-ass guesses). No matter. If "it"—any "it"—on the timeline looks insane/impossible/ridiculous, you've got a potentially b-i-g problem on your hands. Think about it.

2. Timelines-in-the-near-term are cast in stone. A promise of a milestone to be made three weeks hence … is a **promise.** *But* they—milestones—are also obviously flexible. (Things *do* change.) So keep *every* timeline. (Play Historian and Project Conscience.) *But* update regularly; every, say, week. (At a specified time.)

3. Post the current timeline-milestone "list" … IN BIG PRINT … prominently. (As well as electronically.) The idea of the timeline is as much psychological—urgency engendering—as it is rational.

3a. Redux: *Beware of "sophisticated" planning software. (Again.) Like spreadsheets, it makes you feel smart … when you're not. A lot of the power of the timeline is its stark simplicity. Message No. 1:* DON'T GARBAGE IT UP!

40a.

The Nub

My wife and I are in the waning moments of a building project. More or less. And it's the "less" part of "more or less" that's the problem!

That is, we've been stuck at "98 percent complete"... for months.

Which reminded me anew how much every project needs a "Ms. Last Two Percent."

It's (she's) a bit like the Timeline Tyrant identified above. But also different: This is a specialism!

Truth is, I love "last two percent" work. Those last three passes through a manuscript ... in which every word change carries great weight; you f-i-n-a-l-l-y figure out how to say whatever "just right."

Or: You catch that incredibly embarrassing error ... that would have killed you if it had made it into print.

Or: You switch two chapters around ... and the whole argument makes much more sense. Or ...

If you "love it," you're golden. If last-two-percentism is an annoyance, you're ... in my book ... in trouble. That is ...

Last Two Percent Fanaticism is what often separates a "pretty good job" from a "WOW."

"Finishers" are gems of human beings! Every project needs one!

T.T.D./Finisher Power!

1. Acknowledge the issue ... the opportunity ... and the fact that "it" is not everyone's cup of tea.

2. Recruit Ms. Last Two Percent! Ask around: Seek out a proven finisher.

3. Protect Ms. Last Two Percent from charges of "hopeless nitpicker." (That's what she's here for!)

4. Reward Ms. Last Two Percent as a full-scale teammate. (Just as baseball teams reward their "closers." Some—like former Oakland A's reliever Dennis Eckersley—were winners of the coveted Cy Young award, as best pitcher in the league.)

41.

A "must-attend," 15-minutes-*maximum* 8 a.m. meeting—in which we surface the day's milestones, needs for assistance, snafus—can make all the difference.

Also, when a crunch arises during the day: Call a "15-minute meeting"… and sort it out.

If you are religious about adhering to the "Fifteen Max" rule, you'll discover you've stumbled across a powerful implementation device!

The Nub

The 15-minute-maximum meeting adds another stake to my "It's simplicity, stupid" mantra/campaign. I've watched this process up close at CNN. And heard about it at the old/fabled Lockheed Skunk Works. And… tried it myself. And… rammed it down others' throats. In short:

It works.

When people have 15 minutes to get things covered, they get things covered in 15 minutes. There's no room for fat, for pontificating, for unnecessary deference. People learn to state their cases simply and succinctly (an extra skill-building benefit). Gone are all the small, time-wasting rituals that turn too many meetings into endless drones. The 15-minute-maximum-meeting routine sends powerful messages about *action ... clarity ... brevity ... focus ... simplicity.*

Of course, the project management architecture will demand meetings of all sorts. But this one is in a class by itself: *the* day-starter meeting ... an incredibly *brief* ... **sacred** ... event which surfaces as many "what's-going-on" issues as possible ... at lightning speed ... and disposes of them ... at lightning speed.

T.T.D./ **Lightning Speed** Standup Meetings

1. So... **do it/schedule it**—your first "Standup 15 Meeting" (15 minutes, standing up)—in the next 24 hours. (And, say, every 24 or 48 hours thereafter.) Agenda: **(1)** What's happened in the last 24 hours. **(2)** What's going on today. And **(3)** nothing else!

2. Never go to 16 minutes. (Fourteen is just great, though.) **USE AN EGG TIMER.**

3. When you're absent (project manager) ... delegate. I.e.: Have the meeting if only 3 folks—of 14—are in town. **BUT HAVE THE MEETING! RELIGIOUSLY!** Make it clear—as in "What part of 'no' don't you understand?"— that *nobody* misses this meeting. (Period.)

42.

No event or accomplishment is too small to warrant a small celebration. The idea is to keep the troops pumped … and to keep the buzz-z-z-z buzzing in the larger world.

The Nub

Execution—of anything WOW-worthy—is tough. Unexpected setbacks: The material doesn't arrive … a "supporter" turns against you … a key teammate is called to another assignment just when you need her most.

Upshot: As in the endless 162-game regular Major League Baseball season, the manager's (in our case the project manager's) main role is to keep enthusiasm from flagging.

In short: The best project managers are shameless enthusiasts. ("I am a dispenser of enthusiasm"—Benjamin Zander, esteemed conductor, Boston Philharmonic … and renowned management guru.) They look for the flimsiest excuse to … c-e-l-e-b-r-a-t-e/praise/acclaim/applaud/cheer … to pump up the troops.

"Dispenser of Enthusiasm": That's the (exact) ticket! Does it describe you? If "yes" … are you sure? If "no" … what do you plan to do about it? In the next two *hours*? (Personality is probably important; but it's my observation that you *can* learn to be an enthusiast ... e.g., can learn the Habit of Spontaneous Celebration.)

T.T.D./ Enthusiast-in-Chief!

1. What—*specifically*—have you done in the last

2/12/24/48 hours

to "pump up the troops"? (If nothing ... for shame!)

2. Do you instinctively— **d a i l y !** —look for opportunities to celebrate s-o-m-e-t-h-i-n-g ... no matter how small?

3. Are you "Master of T-shirts"? Master of: pens ... banners ... goodies-for-lead-customers? Master of: all-things-symbolic that help move the project forward? Hint again: **This trait <u>can</u> be learned!**

4. Within the next 48 hours, deliver to your gang some physical symbol (how about a cake shaped like ... your project?) of their great work and your WOW Project.

42a.

CELEBRATE FAILURES!

Remember: Product-design guru David Kelley says, "Reward success and failure equally. Punish inactivity." This is easy to write, hard-as-the-devil for many traditionalists to grasp—and act upon.

The Nub

It is axiomatic. If the Quick Prototype is the reigning religion ... then Quick Screwup is the obvious—and sought-after—saint. (Well, Quick Triumph is the real saint, but Quick Screwup is certainly saintly ... in pursuit of Quick Triumph.)

It *is* axiomatic: Quick Trials breed Quick Failures. Which—of course— breed Quick Adjustments. Which—of course—breed Quick Successes. *Which is the whole-damn-idea!*

And: absent in most—*98 percent? (truly)*—big organizations.

So ... no baloney ... **C-E-L-E-B-R-A-T-E THOSE QUICK FAILURES!** Remember that seminal rendition, courtesy of Sydney seminar participant Phil Daniels: *Reward* ... excellent/noble/honest/Cool ... failures! *Punish* ... *mediocre successes!*

WOW Projects are the precise opposite of "mediocre successes." And, truth be known, the search/reach/push-for-WOW can and will lead to ... yes ... project failure(s). But—in my book—far better a Reach-for-WOW-That-Bombs ... than months (years?) spent on a non-WOW, non-memorable "success." So celebrate those overreaches ... products of Zeal-for-Excellence-That-Goeth-Awry. (And ... sometimes ... *badly* awry.)

т.т.d./**Embrace** Failures!

1. Have you (project/unit boss) given accolades—*this month*—to team members who reached for the stars ... and bumped their heads? This is not a joke ... or an approximation:

I AM TALKING ABOUT CELEBRATING "EXCELLENT" SCREWUPS! E-X-P-L-I-C-I-T-L-Y!

2. Consider a weekly "Best Screwup" award. E.g.: a **bronzed screw,** which is retained by the recipient for the week. *Why not?*

3. Tell Stories ... publicly, regularly ... about reaching-for-the-stars, even though it **(regularly)** means setbacks **(and sometimes b-i-g setbacks)** along the way. Do you let it be known in no uncertain terms that you're aware these setbacks will occur; that, in fact, you welcome/honor/**c h e r i s h**/ c-e-l-e-b-r-a-t-e them?

43.

STATION BREAK!
THE KEYNOTE HERE IS ACTION.
EXACTLY RIGHT!
BUT: DON'T ALLOW THE
ACTION FANATICISM TO
STEER YOU OFF COURSE
RE WOW!/BEAUTY!/REVOLUTION!/
IMPACT!/RAVING FANS!

While championing blinding speed, keep raising the WOW! ante at every turn. E.g.: *Every* quick prototype *must be* a Beautiful/WOW! quick prototype! Also: Take the group away for a day now and then to reflect on the over-arching principles of WOW, and keep asking that respected elder/advisor:

"DOES 'IT' STILL SMELL 'WOW'?"

The Nub

Message: Never—*ever!*—neglect: WOW/BEAUTY/REVOLUTIONARY/RAVING FANS/IMPACT. The bias of this "implementation" section is speed/action: Try it! Test it! Screw it up! Adjust it! N-O-W!

And I stand—squarely!—behind that bias as Implementer's Rule No. 1.

Still: In the haste to test-adjust-test, don't let WOW! (etc.) inadvertently slip into the background.

It *is* the easiest thing to do. You're hustling to beat the band. And the successful trials are rolling in. BUT...IS IT STILL **COOL-BEYOND-BELIEF?** Because if it ain't...all the speed in the world will leave you running in place! Get back to first principles (per this book): Stay in touch with the Mother Lode/Inspiration/WOW! at any and all costs.

T.T.D./Remember WOW!

1. Talk up WOW e-v-e-r-y d-a-y. No kidding! **(Damn it.)**

2. Write WOW Reminders (e.g., regular e-mail) that get everyone re-focused on the WOW dimension...no matter how pressing their immediate milestones.

3. At the halfway mark in the project...**take the whole team away** ... and ask them whether or not the project should be continued.

I.e.: **Will it WOW?!**

44.

So … actively encourage that "project personality."

The Nub

Identity-Is-All. That's what the savvy marketers tell us … to explain the lasting success of Coke … IBM … BMW … and the new successes of Starbucks … Nike … Intel.

But is "identity" limited to the branding of Big Corp.? I don't think so. In fact, I think that creating (and maintaining) identity—in the Starbucks/BMW fashion—is near the heart of "implementation excellence" for the WOW Project Champion/Project Manager. (Though, God knows—**as usual!**—you'll not find a hint of the idea in any project management "guide"/"handbook"!)

WOW Project = Character = Personality = Brand = Identity.

T.T.D./Identity! Character!

1. What's going on here? What are we trying to do? **WHAT DO WE STAND FOR?** Work—assiduously— on these questions. They are a big part of "mundane" implementation. After all: To what end "implementation," if not to Stand-for-Something-Distinct/Big?

2. *What* **is** *identity?* Talk to your team about it ... in general ... in the context of your WOW-to-be project.

3. Call a friend—or a friend of a friend—who is an "identity consultant." Invite her/him to lunch. Have her/him talk to you and your gang about identity in Starbucks's terms ... as it could apply to your "mundane" project. (Recall my bias: *No* project needs to be "mundane." All/any can be the thin-end-of-the-wedge-for-transformation-and-WOW!")

4. Selfishly: See our forthcoming *the Design+ Identity50*. (We've included it in this series precisely because we fervently believe that Identity—project, individual—is imperative to New World Order Success ... where Stand Out or Stand Down is the inescapable Mantra-Axiom.)

45.

Eventually you have to go more or less mainstream. Not too soon. But eventually.

That is ... you need to start tantalizing The Suits, too.

Broadcast—somewhat—success stories from your road tests as they roll in. Conduct a few "public" briefings. Add some Suits to your growing, increasingly inclusive Advisory Board.

The Nub

As the project succeeds, you must shed (ironically) the in-your-face, revolutionary skin and embrace **(yes ... embrace!)** the "enemy"/suits. The net must be cast unflinchingly—and gracefully!—toward yesterday's Doubting (Pissed-Off-at-You) Thomases.

It's simple: If your "it"/your "baby" is to go "mainstream" then, hey, you **must** enthusiastically ally with the "mainstream."

Period.

T.T.D./Romance "The Suits"!

1. Change your stripes. Down comes the pirate flag. **We're goin' mainstream, baby!**

2. Literally: Concoct a formal—rigorous/vigorous!—Plan to Market to The Suits. E.g.: Start with a series of briefings—**25 in 25 days?!**—to share your (now-mostly-developed) stuff with the mainstreamers/accountants/systems freaks; invite them in for demos (and take your show on the road ... i.e., take the demos to them).

3. Add Suits to your team! Okay ... "they" snubbed you just three months ago. Tough! You need them ... now.

So recruit them ...

love them ...

use them ...

let them use you ...

co-opt them ...

make them feel "part of the family"
(even if it makes you want to heave!).

46.

THE EVENTUAL IMPLEMENTATION KEY
IS *NOT* SELLING THE HIGHER-UPS; IT IS
HAVING EARLY USERS PUBLICLY *BEGGING*
FOR MORE ... MORE ... MORE. BEGGING
SO LOUDLY THAT THE HIGHER-UPS CAN'T
IGNORE THEM (OR Y-O-U!).

E.g.: Work proactively on "word-of-mouth marketing"
from literal day No. 1. Collect and publicize "little" success stories and testimonials. (Hint: Good stories =
Good marketing.)

The Nub

Message:
**"Implementation" success is early custo-
mers who love us and love our "it" and will
create Glowing Testimonials to that effect.**

I'm so irritated! (Redux!) Early-customers-
as-our-chief-spokespeople is simply not part of the
"project management" literature. Again: How unspeak-
ably stupid!

At this point in our WOW Project, we are in an all-out, no-baloney, expansion-sales mode. Expanding our net of supporters. And working on our network of users, too.

We now need a teammate (one … or more) who "runs" our budding User Community.

We now need to get organized around broad-based user-community building.

T.T.D./Users-as-Extroverted-Fans!

1. Schedule a User Group Meeting … **today.** Begin to turn your users into a noisy-but-organized Cheerleading Section as you expand your project's reach. Appoint someone on the team—or bring in someone new—to be the User Group Maven. I.e.:

Formalize and systematize the process.

2. U-s-e the User Group! This is "sales" … sure. But you are also entering the refinement stage. The dozens of little improvements that real/mainstream users recommend will mean the difference between success … and failure … for the whole project. (Yes, abject failure—or "Mediocre success"—is still a possibility. Don't forget it!) Once again: *Systematize* this process of getting/absorbing user input.

47

Alas, most don't see it that way. "Staffers" usually follow the "If-we-build-it-they-will-come" approach. Disastrous!

The key idea redux: **Buzz doesn't build automatically.** But it *can* be nudged into existence—via time spent if not $$$$$. No formal B.M.P.… no buzz-z-z-z-z.

The Nub

Now—as the implementation phase becomes more and more robust—we are talking no-holds-barred marketing. Marketing qua marketing.

Without marketing, you are n-o-t-h-i-n-g.

Marketing/P.R./Buzz/Word-of-Mouth is obviously a professional discipline in its own right. Has the time come to hire—or scrounge – a "real," full-time marketing exec for the project's final push? Perhaps!

One common lesson that can be gleaned from "teams" research: Different sorts of leaders are required at different phases of the program/project. Maybe now is the time to assign de facto leadership to the team's marketing guru-in-waiting … or an outsider brought in to pursue the same task. THINK—LONG AND HARD—ABOUT IT!

T.T.D./Buzz!

1. Study rollouts of Great Projects/Products: Apple's first Mac … Windows95 … Gillette's MACH3 … VW's new Beetle. Take marketing/buzz/word-of-mouth seriously … as a strategic issue demanding your rapt attention. This issue is legitimate—not "smoke and mirrors" —and begs to be considered thoughtfully.

2. Appoint (or acquire) a Buzz Manager. (Now.)

3. Develop a formal Marketing/Buzz Plan … even if this is a six-week project. (No matter: Sales *is* s-t-i-l-l it!) Be as imaginative/energetic in creating your Buzz Management Program as you were about the "it" of the project per se. This is where the whole shebang could fall apart … if you are not v-e-r-y serious. And v-e-r-y attentive.

REPRISE:
IMPLEMENTATION
MY BREAKOUT
WOW PROJECT

At McKinsey & Co., I was the guy who had the silly little project. It turned into *In Search of Excellence*. (And a huge program/core competence for McKinsey.) Here's my take on it, with the benefit of hindsight:

1. Be naïve. Nothing counts so much as ignorance—even if it's willful. It's what the Zen practitioners call cultivating "beginner's mind." I was really starting fresh ... in terms of "making something happen" at McKinsey. Knowing what I know now about McKinsey, I would never have accepted the assignment. (Thank God I didn't know what I didn't know.)

2. Y-o-u gotta believe ... and have a cause! I really believed in the meat of my organizational effectiveness project. And I really believed that McKinsey was doing it all wrong—i.e., far too much emphasis on strategy, far too little on organizational cultures and implementation.

3. Be prepared to take some shit. I was battered by some of McKinsey's best and brightest... and most powerful. I am ordinarily a wimp...but I bought my own act (I loved what I was doing!), so I hung in. (For four years ... then ... enough was enough.)

4. You—desperately—need a couple of buddies. I had o-n-e really good pal. (Allan Kennedy.)

He was smarter than Hell, and his support—and belief in me and the substance of the project—made all the difference.

5. I worked my ass off. The weirdo/subversive—me, in this case—has to appear tougher and toil harder than his/her opponents.

6. Cast the net widely. Another McKinsey mentor, Allen Puckett, taught me to seek allies from (very) far and (very) wide. I had a great set of Weird Supporters. It helped—a lot.

7. To make a b-i-g difference you've got to reframe the issue. *I/we ended up redefining the basic idea of "organizational effectiveness" within the context of McKinsey's practice ... and, to some extent, the world at large.*

8. It's gotta cohere. Helped (a lot!) by my friend and boss, Bob Waterman, we concocted and communicated an understandable paradigm. (I hate the general overuse of the term, but I think it's merited here.) We put together a "coherent model"—the so-called "McKinsey 7-S Framework"—that mainstream people in the firm could understand ... and use. (And still use ... 20 years later!)

9. Iterate. I kept playing ... and playing. I never pretended I had it right.

10. Go public ... early. It was scary as hell ... but early on I/we let it all hang out ... in public ... via published articles and seminars. We took some hits. But we learned a lot. Fast. (Understatement.)

11. Build a network of the "powerless." Some of "my" early supporters are now famous men and women. At the time, they weren't. My point: Find "cool," committed people. Don't worry whether they're powerful or not.

12. Recruit ... ad nauseam. To get my ideas "into the system" I had to be in a de facto constant recruiting mode. Only by weaving a worldwide spider's web would there be any chance of a legacy.

13. Far away = Good. I was 3,000 miles from headquarters (San Francisco vs. New York). It helped!

14. Cherish the "underdog" mentality. There was another parallel project at McKinsey that was a (much) bigger deal. So ... little was expected of us. That was an advantage. (We sneaked up on the bastards!)

15. Stick your neck w-a-y out. We put on a big show—a five-day seminar involving some very senior folks—pretty early in the project's life. It was a **B-I-G** risk. And worth it. (In hindsight.) We showed we were real/solid/exciting enough to get some important people's attention.

16. Seek good cover. I would not have survived unless I'd had good cover ... namely Bob Waterman, a quirky but Establishment guy.

17. Don't be a jerk. I was on a mission. I was a believer. I rejected conventional wisdom ... in a v-e-r-y proud institution. But I received good counsel: BE NICE! That is, don't be sore—or take it personally

—when things don't go your way. Take the heat that's gonna come if you're on to something. Be the first one at the meeting … conservatively dressed, polite, etc. (At times it wasn't easy … i.e., when someone I didn't respect wanted my scalp. And, hey, eventually I became a jerk— to the establishment—about my project. And I left. Translation: Was pushed.)

18. Sympathy at the top doesn't hurt. If we had failed, few tears would have been shed. On the other hand, the two (big) guys at the top—Ron Daniel and War-ren Cannon—were sympathetic to our/my cause.

* * *

There's much more to the story, of course. But these are a few highlights … that underscore many of the main messages of this section.

IV. exit!

IV. A time to each and every thing!

Mr. Gingrich moved history.... Tons of guts is part of what got him to the speakership, along with an almost deranged optimism and imagination.... [His] vision of himself was so shaped by his differentness, his outsiderness, that he couldn't get it through his head that he was now an insider.

—*Wall Street Journal,* November 9, 1998, on Newt Gingrich resigning the Speakership

The architect-builder of the Channel Tunnel is hardly likely to be its best director of operations. That's obvious. So, too, with most any project: The enthusiast-dreamer-salesperson-relentless-prototyper is likely to be a lousy candidate for day-to-day oversight, or for taking responsibility for the superfine-tuning needed to make all the systems pieces fit together. Hence, there is a time to celebrate Success ... turn over the reins ... quit ... refresh ... and get out and get on with the Next Impossible Dream ... a.k.a. WOW Project.

48.

It's been "us" against "them" ... and one heck of a ride. But now the time has come to dance with the Suits if we really want full impact. You must morph from firebrand/queen-of-quick-and-dirty to empathetic listener/ systems, procedures, and infrastructure champion.

I.e.: (1) **You gotta make nice to the people who may have been obstructing you/ dissing you for the last eight months;** (2) **You gotta learn to love the procedure manuals that lock your project into concrete. Remember: Real/Sustained success = Locking into the mainstream.**

In startup land, this is the wrenching transition from "entrepreneurial" management to "professional" management. Not many make the transition easily. Which may mean: Time for another Supreme Commander.

The Nub

Turn the other cheek! Your baby—your WOW Project —will only have lasting impact if it leaves your nurturing nest and makes its mark in the mainstream. The revolutionary's prickly skin must be exchanged for the administrator's silkier skin. **THIS IS A F-A-C-T.**

191

T.T.D./Gliding into the Mainstream

1. Expand the team. Again. *And* again. And then again. Bring in the "systems guys." Start working

assiduously!

on the development of procedure manual/documentation that will smooth the widespread adoption of your "deliverables" into the company's daily procedures.

2. Make—**good!**—pals in IS. In HR. In Finance. In … whatever. Pave the way for a whole new phase of the project. Shift your "lunch strategy" (time spent recruiting supporters) from freaks and renegades to pure, unadulterated establishment types.

3. Recruit slightly renegade "leaders" in each of the key areas—HR, IS, Finance, etc.—who will become the new shepherds of your project in this next—crucial!—phase.

DO NOT CON YOURSELF INTO BELIEVING THAT THE PIRATE/IN-YOUR-FACE TEAM (INCLUDING YOU) CAN PULL THIS OFF.

HINT: **YOU CAN'T!**

48a.

The Nub

At the pinnacle of "big business" it's called "succession planning." It is often done poorly ... ignored until the last minute ... or hopelessly politicized. And yet it is no stretch to say it is the key to your legacy!

Hence my heartfelt advice: Take "succession planning" seriously. (It's as important for the WOW Project as it is for the corporation looking for a new CEO.) Spend time on it ... big time. Seek—far and wide and bold—a follow-up chief, with your abiding passion and the right skills for the next phase of the project's life. Delay your departure until you've done your utmost to ensure a fabulous transition.

T.T.D./Finding: My Brilliant Successor!

1. Put your entire energy into finding an inspired successor as your own "era" draws—as it must—to a close.

2. Study succession planning. Talk to consultants who specialize in it.

3. Hang in ... until you get it "right." Or ... as right as you can.

Again:

This is a Big Deal.
It takes Time ...
Imagination ...
Political Skill ...
Emotional Energy ...
And: A dose of Ego-less-ness.
(Gobs of each!)

49.

SEED YOUR FREAKS INTO THE MAINSTREAM . . . WHERE THEY CAN BECOME MUTANT VIRUSES FOR YOUR (QUIRKY) POINT OF VIEW!

The Nub

There are two h-u-g-e ideas here:

(1) Take care of "your" troops. They are proud, scarred vets. Make sure they land on their feet!

(2) Follow the guidelines of my revolutionary U.S. Air Force pal, the former head of the Tactical Air Command, General Bill Creech:

SPEND A L-O-T OF TIME PLACING YOUR FREAKS/MUTANTS/WOW-VIRUS CARRIERS INTO POSITIONS AROUND THE FIRM WHERE THEY CAN SPREAD THE FREAKY NEW GOSPEL.

T.T.D./ Sow the seeds!

1. Work (long and hard) with your whole network to find spots for *each* of your team members.

Key spots. Maybe not "power" slots ... but high-leverage slots where they can spread their (your!) wild message far *and* wide. (Hint: One of the fab side benefits: You get the rep as a "guy who takes care of his troops." This helps —immeasurably!—when you go begging for help in the future. And you will!)

    2. *THIS IS D-A-M-N IMPORTANT.*

AND COMMONLY IGNORED.

Blow this one ... and long-term project impact ... even at this late date ... will be savaged.

50.

Send 100—or 250 or 2,500—"thank you" notes. (Never lose sight of "the network"!)

Confer blessings on your successor. Take a few days (weeks!) off.

And then ... start all over again.

Such is the life of the All-Star WOW Project Pro.

The Nub

Party time!

Celebrate! Rejoice! Write up the team's history! Concoct the photo album! Rest! Relax!

(And ... then ... start all over again!)

T.T.D./Celebrate and Skedaddle!

Plan—carefully—a monster celebratory bash. Or a series of celebratory bashes.

Lavish credit on anyone and everyone ... who helped you the least bit.

Create a blossoming aura of goodwill ... and inevitability ... around your project.

Then ... after playing Taps ... go. Quickly. Graciously.

(YOUR TIME HAS COME AND ...
PROBABLY ... PASSED.)

AFTERWORD:
PRESENT AT THE
CREATION?

In the movie *Patton,* actor George C. Scott stands before an enormous American flag exhorting would-be Army recruits. "And when your boy asks you," he bellows at one point, "'Daddy, what did you do during the Great World War II?' you won't have to say, 'I was shoveling shit in Louisiana!'"

I worked up a near-Pattonian/Scottian rage myself, in the fall of 1998, talking to thousands of information-systems managers engaged in the installation of ERP/Enterprise Resource Planning systems. These systems, I vowed, are the engine of the encompassing white collar revolution. Yet most of the projects these folks were engaged in were rather timid—or, at least, a long way from the potential the system has.

And so I recalled the Patton/Scott lines (matched Scott's bellow, truth be known), and then asked, "And when your son or daughter asks you, 'Daddy, what did you do during the Great Twenty-first Century Competitiveness Revolution?' are you going to have to say, 'I was shoveling old paradigm shit in [no city will be trashed here]?'"

* * *

That is:
Where the Hell's the W-O-W?

I know all the excuses—internal politics, dreary boss, etc.—but none is relevant, as I see it. "You are the blessed ones," I concluded, "the information-systems professionals who hold the key to the strongbox. It is your game to play or not to play … to win or to lose. Will you stride boldly into a future of your own design? Will you WOW? Or will you sit on the sidelines, producing 'mediocre successes,' while the once-every-five-hundred-years revolution passes you by?"

The Movement!

How audacious! Start a Movement?! We plan to do just that.

Title: The Work Matters!

Or: The Anti-Dilbert Movement.

We are sick and tired of whining about lousy bosses. (Or companies.) It is—as we see it—our life. To live … or lose. To form … or allow to be formed.

Dilbert is hilarious.(I.e., on the money.) And there's the rub. Dilbert stands not only for cynicism (an emotion I appreciate) but also for the de facto acceptance of power-less-ness. Power-less-ness … at the coolest time in centuries to make a mark. And that is where I draw the line!

It is my life. To live … fully. Or not. And I damn well intend to live it fully. And I don't think I'm alone.

So my colleagues and I are … audaciously … starting a Movement:

The Work Matters!

And we invite you to join us. Cost of membership: the time it takes to type **www.tompeters.com** into your browser.

Welcome aboard!

(P.S.: You may have noted the oversized  in the paragraphs above. No accident. That is our symbol ... the exclamation point...about as far from Dilbert as one can get, eh?)

www.tompeters.com

READING AND VIEWING RESOURCES

WOW stories. As you know by now, "project management literature" is not my cup of tea. But there *is* a **terrific** "project literature"—WOW stories. E.g....

ORGANIZING GENIUS: THE SECRETS OF CREATIVE COLLABORATION, by Warren Bennis and Patricia Ward Biederman (Reading, MA: Addison-Wesley, 1977). Brilliant, humanistic analysis of the Lockheed Skunk Works, the Disney Feature Animation Unit, and other "Great Groups in Pursuit of WOW Projects," as the authors label them.

HOT GROUPS: SEEDING THEM, FEEDING THEM, AND USING THEM TO IGNITE YOUR ORGANIZATION, by Jean Lipman-Blumen and Harold Leavitt (London: Oxford University Press, 1999). A close—and rare—kin to the Bennis-and-Biederman book. Hot Groups doing Hot Work. The bedrock of Work in the new millennium!

THE SOUL OF A NEW MACHINE, by Tracy Kidder (Boston: Little, Brown, 1981). This classic follows the day-to-day development of a new computer at Data General. For a précis, see Chapter 10 of my *A Passion for Excellence.* Also see Kidder's wonderful *House* (Boston: Houghton Mifflin, 1985).

THE MAKING OF THE ATOMIC BOMB, by Richard Rhodes (New York: Simon & Schuster, 1986). A giant page-turner tracks the Mother of All Projects: the Manhattan Project.

THE INVENTION THAT CHANGED THE WORLD: HOW A SMALL GROUP OF RADAR PIONEERS WON THE SECOND WORLD WAR AND LAUNCHED A TECHNOLOGICAL REVOLUTION, by Robert Buderi (New York: Simon & Schuster, 1996). Close kin to the bomb book.

747: STORY OF THE BOEING SUPER JET, by Douglas Ingells (Fallbrook, CA: Aero Publishers, 1970). Talk about drama! (And a WOW Project!)

ENDURANCE: SHACKLETON'S INCREDIBLE VOYAGE, by Alfred Lansing (Carroll & Gray, 1999). The tales of the Antarctic and Arctic explorers are true WOW Project stories. The aspiration. The "sales job." The politics. The making of a Team. The ecstasy. The agony. This book about Sir Ernest Shackleton's Antarctic journey tops my list. Also see *The Worst Journey in the World,* by Apsley Cherry-Garrard (Carroll & Gray, 1997), about Robert Falcon Scott's last Antarctic journey. And, on a related note: *Into Thin Air,* by John Krakauer (New York: Anchor Books, 1999); again, the Devil is in the Details ... and the Politics ... and the Passion in making and breaking WOW Projects, in their case a 1996 assault on Mount Everest.

THE DEVIL'S CANDY: THE BONFIRE OF THE VANITIES GOES TO HOLLYWOOD, by Julie Salamon (Boston: Houghton Mifflin, 1991). Learn *lots* from a fiasco of a project—Hollywood style.

LEONARD BERNSTEIN: REACHING FOR THE NOTE, videorecording directed by Susan Lacy, 1998.

About someone who always reached for WOW in his projects, often fell short... but was nonetheless music's man-of-the-century.

* * *

General. Books on political and military campaigns fill our bill, too. The point: Such writing chronicles the WOW!, the heartbreak, the human dimension ... which is notably absent in almost all "formal"—and largely counterproductive—project/project management literature. E.g....

THE MAKING OF THE PRESIDENT 1960, by Theodore Harold White (New York: Atheneum Publishers, 1961).(See also *The Making of the President 1964, 1968,* and *1972.*)

PRIMARY COLORS: A NOVEL OF POLITICS, by Anonymous ... a.k.a. Joe Klein (New York: Random House, 1996). Forget your view of Our Man in the White House; he got there ... and you and I didn't ... and the process was a WOW Project.(Right?)

THE WAR ROOM [videorecording]/Pennebaker Associates Inc. & McEttinger Films, Inc., Vidmark Entertainment, 1994. James Carville ... up close and personal.

ALL'S FAIR: LOVE, WAR, AND RUNNING FOR PRESIDENT, by Mary Matalin and James Carville, with Peter Knobler (New York: Random House, 1994).

PATTON [videorecording]/Twentieth-Century Fox; screen story and screenplay by Francis Ford Coppola and

Edmund H. North; directed by Franklin J. Schaffner. Patton was a helluva WOW Project guy … though a little weak on political skills!

THE RICKOVER EFFECT: HOW ONE MAN MADE A DIFFERENCE, by Theodore Rockwell (Annapolis, MD: Naval Institute Press, 1992). The making of the nuclear navy was one Hell of a ride!

DOC: THE STORY OF DENNIS LITTKY AND HIS FIGHT FOR A BETTER SCHOOL, by Susan Kammeraad-Campbell (Chicago: Contemporary Books, 1989). Littky's WOW Project at Thayer High in Winchester, NH, is True Grit to the fifth power! (I saw it firsthand.)

* * *

Creativity. WOW Projects are about looking at the world through new lenses. I am not much of a fan of "creativity books." But there are a (very) few exceptions:

AHA!, by Jordan Ayan (New York: Crown, 1997). I must have bent back half the pages of this book … to my own amazement. Likewise, try *How to Think Like Leonardo da Vinci,* by Michael Gelb (New York: Delacorte Press, 1998). Another page-bender!

SERIOUS PLAY, by Michael Schrage (Boston: Harvard Business School Press, 1999). Simply the best book I've ever read on innovation. Main topic: rapid prototyping. A lovely companion is *Deep Play,* by Diane Ackerman (New York: Random House, 1999).

See sources cited at www.tompeters.com.

ACKNOWLEDGMENTS

Paul Ryder@Ninthhouse ... who invented the "Way Cool Project" idea. Julie Anixter ... who said to me, "What are the 50 things you think are most important about projects?" (Hence this series of *50Lists*.) Erik Hansen ... WOW Project Grand Panjandrum for this book and chief architect, along with Julie A., of **The Movement!** Sonny Mehta ... "the publisher" ... who's always up for something new and interesting. Edward Kastenmeier (Knopf) and Sebastian Stuart (himself!) ... for inspired and meticulous editing.

Ken Silvia ... design genius and Mr.! (Eat your heart out, Dilbert.) Alan Webber, who "gets this stuff" more than I do, and Cheryl Dahle at *Fast Company* ... who gave these ideas light-of-day exposure ... Big Time! The WOW-ful Ninth House WOW Projects team, incl.: Laurie Sain, Leslie Mullens, David Spitzer, Robin Harper, Bill O'Connor, Susan Baldwin, and Jeff Snipes. Ron Crossland, Boyd Clarke, Rick King, and Madeleine McGrath at Tom Peters Company ... who got behind the WOW Project Workshop with vigor and imagination. Esther Newberg at ICM ... who pushed the book project with her usual flair and tenacity. Knopf All-World Design Guru Chip Kidd ... who invented the look and feel of this series. Pat Johnson ... believer and Knopf marketing maestro.

Larry Holman, Bunny Holman, Linda Allin, and Joe Brumley at WYNCOM ... for providing the Lessons in Leadership seminar series, the perfect platform for presenting my ideas. Patrik Jonsson and Jim Napolitano at

Mulberry Studio for translating my original hen-scratch-ings—yes, all of my first drafts are Bic on Yellow Pad—into a usable ms. Sue Bencuya ... for fact-checking. Elyse Friedman, Martha Lawler, and Vincent Renstrom ... for editorial expertise. Katherine Hourigan, without whose assistance none of this would actually have happened ... Mel Rosenthal, who helped eliminate errors and inconsistencies ... Andy Hughes and Quinn O'Neill, who turned these words into the bound book you now hold in your hands ... Merri Ann Morrell, whose herculean efforts helped make these books possible. Ian Thomson and Michelle Rotzin ... for minding the store at Tom Peters Company in Palo Alto. Dick Anderson, Allen Puckett, Allan Kennedy, Walt Minnick, Bob Waterman, and the late Blake van Leer ... for teaching me about Cool Projects.

And Susan Sargent ... best friend and mentor ... for living the WOW Projects life at warp speed with guts, grit, and imagination ... and thence serving as role model extraordinaire.

Tom Peters
Cape Poge, Massachusetts
19 July 1999

Tom Peters is the co-author of *In Search of Excellence* (with Robert H. Waterman, Jr.) and *A Passion for Excellence* (with Nancy Austin), and the author of *Thriving on Chaos*, *Liberation Management*, *The Tom Peters Seminar*, *The Pursuit of Wow!*, *The Circle of Innovation*, and the *Reinventing Work* series. He is the founder of the Tom Peters Company, with offices in Palo Alto, Boston, Chicago, Cincinnati, and London. He and his family live on a farm in Vermont and an island off the Massachusetts coast, thanks to the information technology revolution. He can be reached at **tom@tompeters.com.**